WASHINGTON

Here is the story of the land that is Washington and of the people who came to it and made it a great state.

A hundred million years ago the floor of the sea rose and the Olympic Islands became a peninsula. Volcanic action tossed up the Cascades and left thousands of acres covered with lava. Glaciers shaped the land. A drowned Puget Sound was left with 300 mountain-top islands. A rain-drenched coast was cut off by mountains from the drier plains. Mount Rainier beckoned travelers to its 26 glaciers, 62 lakes, and 34 waterfalls.

This rugged, beautiful country was dominated for years by the Hudson's Bay Company, furs, and Dr. John McLoughlin.

The Columbia River cutting through the Cascade and Coast ranges became a thoroughfare for explorers, missionaries, settlers. Later, water-power, lumber, salmon, fertile valleys, brought the people of many nationalities who have made Washington what it is today.

Phil Austin spent several months in Washington capturing the beauty of the state with his water colors.

Enchantment of America

WASHINGTON

FROM ITS GLORIOUS PAST TO THE PRESENT

By Allan Carpenter

Illustrations by Phil Austin

CHILDRENS PRESS

Consultant

Rolland H. Upton, Superintendent
Olympia Public Schools

For their advice and counsel and gracious help the author thanks:

Daniel J. Evans, Governor
Rolland H. Upton, Superintendent, Olympia Public Schools
Ted R. Knightlinger, Manager, Department of Commerce and
    Economic Development
Don Becker, Information Officer, Department of Commerce and
    Economic Development
R. L. Chisholm, Superintendent of Schools, Richland
Tom Balow
Seattle Chamber of Commerce
Spokane Chamber of Commerce
Evanston Public Library

Library of Congress Catalog Card Number: 66–11616

3 4 5 6 7 8 9 10 11 12 13 14 15 16 17 18 19 20 21 22 23 24 25   R   75 74 73 72 71 70 69 68

Contents

A True Story to Set the Scene

Saga of the First Settlers

In 1844 a little group of American settlers reached The Dalles on the Columbia River after a tremendously difficult journey by covered wagon over the Oregon Trail. Rivers and streams had been so flooded that the wearisome journey was much delayed. Supplies had run short. At least twenty families were saved only through the kindness of one of the pioneers—George Washington Bush—who fed and supplied them from his own stores and out of his own pocket.

Now at last they had reached the promised land, only to receive the worst blow of all. They could not settle in what is now Oregon state. Actually they all could settle there except for their friend and bene-factor George Bush and his family. If Bush had tried to settle in any part of Oregon below the Columbia River, the law required that he be whipped out of the territory. Why? Because he was a Negro and Negroes were not permitted to settle in Oregon below the Columbia River. No American settlers at all were allowed to settle in Oregon Territory north of that river.

What were they to do?

Their decision may have changed the course of history by tipping the scales to bring Washington to the United States. The story of George Washington Bush and his friends is a little-known but inspiring example of loyalty and humanitarianism—of the triumph of justice and kindness. It even involves a special act of the Congress of the United States—surely one of the most unusual stories of the enchantment of Washington.

George Washington Bush was born to freedom, probably in Phila-delphia in 1770. His parents were servants of a wealthy shipping com-pany owner named Stevenson. They served the Stevensons so well that they inherited his wealth when both Stevensons had died. George, an only child, was educated among the Quakers but gave up some of his Quaker principles to serve gallantly with Andrew Jackson in the Battle of New Orleans in the War of 1812.

Adventurous George Bush next became a voyageur for fur-trading companies, finally with the Hudson's Bay Company. He traveled

9

throughout the West and even reached the Pacific coast. After returning east and farming in several states, he settled down in Clay County, Missouri, married, had five sons, and increased his fortune by industry and intelligent farming.

Prosperity did not protect him from race prejudice, and at length Bush decided to leave all his many comforts and travel to the Oregon Territory where he hoped his children might have a greater chance for happiness. It is probable that George Bush was the wealthiest pioneer to make the overland trip. He carried with him large supplies of nursery stock, seeds, farm implements and livestock. It is said that he nailed a hundred pounds of silver into a false bottom of his wagon. Out of his own pocket he provided money and teams for several of his neighbors who could not otherwise have afforded the trip.

His good and devoted friend, Michael T. Simmons, along with James McAllister, David Kindred, Gabriel Jones, their wives, children, and three bachelors, made up the party. They joined others, making a total group of eighty wagons.

When they reached The Dalles and found that George Bush was not welcome in the American settlements of Oregon Territory, the members of the Bush-Simmons party indignantly agreed not to desert him. For almost a year they camped east of Fort Vancouver on the Washougal River while they tried to decide what to do. Dr. John McLoughlin, who "ruled" the entire Oregon country for the Hudson's Bay Company, had been forbidden to help Americans settle north of the Columbia. But the kindly doctor would not let a man of George Bush's character suffer. In July of 1845, Mike Simmons explored the Puget Sound region and found a place for settlement. For fifteen days the Bush-Simmons party cut a wagon road through the wilderness from Cowlitz Landing to the south end of the Sound. They carried with them a request from Dr. McLoughlin for Hudson's Bay Company men in the region to help them in any way they could.

Simmons felt that the Deschutes River offered a fine location for farming and milling; he took a claim there, and the Bush family settled nearby on 640 acres of level land and called Bush Prairie ever since that time. Others of the party settled within a six-mile circle in what has come to be known as Tumwater. This was the first permanent American settlement in the present state of Washington.

The British had expected to hold all of the Oregon Territory north and west of the Columbia. The settlement of thirty-two Americans in that region may have been the deciding factor in their willingness to settle for the present boundaries. That community of Tumwater, of course, would not have been there at that time if it had not been for George Bush, who by his kindness and character held the loyalty of his friends and may thereby have changed the course of history.

The troubles of George Bush were far from over, however. When Washington became part of Oregon Territory, ironically he became subject once more to the law forbidding Negro settlement. However, Mike Simmons traveled to Oregon City and pleaded his friend's case so well that a special law was passed by the Territorial Legislature exempting Bush from the anti-Negro law. The family prospered due to Bush's resources and his brilliant management. His gardens flourished; fat stock roamed his pastures; an orchard and large wheat fields added to the abundance. He helped others with seed and stock, and provided the capital for Mike Simmons to build the first sawmill on Puget Sound.

A sixth son was born to the Bush's. So they say that the first "white" child born in Washington was a Negro, meaning, of course, the first non-Indian.

During the winter of 1852, in a time of near famine, George Bush possessed the only food surplus in the whole region. He might have sold this to speculators, but he refused a fortune and gave his wheat and other food to all those who needed it, without taking a penny for his help.

George Bush was never secure in all this success because he could not make legal claim to the land he had worked for so hard. No Negro was permitted by U.S. law to hold title to what was called "Donation" land. However, when later settlers tried to take his land away, the friends of George Bush rallied with a tremendous uproar.

The first Washington Territorial Legislature passed a memorial to Congress which read in part: ". . . by constant and laborious cultivation of said claim and by an accommodating and charitable disposal of his produce to immigrants, he had contributed much toward the settlement of this Territory, the suffering and needy never having applied to him in vain . . . your memorialists are of the opinion that the case is of such meritorious nature that Congress ought to pass a special law donating to him his said claim."

Surprisingly, Congress did respond and passed a special law on January 30, 1855, permitting Bush and his family to keep their property. George Washington Bush died in 1863 at the age of ninety-three, a respected Washington pioneer and humanitarian. His family carried on in the same tradition. The oldest son, W. O. Bush, won first prize for his wheat at the Philadelphia World's Fair in 1876, beating all of the world's other wheat, and the property remained in the Bush family into modern times.

In a time of dissension and doubt, it is reassuring to recall this capable, kindly man who never passed by an opportunity to serve his fellow man. His friends in return, through every difficulty that beset him, refused to desert him until they all triumphed in the end.

Lay of the Land

Molded by Mighty Forces

At some time in the ancient past most of what is Washington today did not even exist. Great oceans swept across the spot where now mighty mountains stand. At one time the present Blue Mountains stood out as headlands on the shore of an ancient sea. Far away to the northwest was a group of islands which are now the Olympic Mountains. Between these two mountain groups was nothing but sparkling water.

Many times the level of the land rose and fell. Mountains were pushed up by mighty pressures from below the surface, then were worn away by winds and waters of the ages. More recently, but still as much as a hundred million years ago, the forces at work below the ground shoved into the air a mighty mountain range we know today as the Cascades. The floor of the sea was also raised and the Olympic Islands were connected to the mainland.

From time to time the great heat and pressures of earth's interior burst forth violently creating ancient volcanoes. From openings in the earth flowed tremendous quantities of lava, covering more than 200,000 square miles. This red-hot molten rock spread itself across the land in such unbelievable abundance that lava-covered regions are a mile thick in some parts of eastern Washington. One evidence of the work of volcanoes is the Channeled Scablands—2,500 square miles of bare lava, the channels gouged by ancient rivers no longer flowing.

Most dramatic reminders of volcanic activity, of course, are the mightiest mountains of Washington—Rainier, Adams, Baker, Glacier Peak, and St. Helens. These were built to great heights by prehistoric lava flows. Later, some lost a part of their height. Mt. Rainier blew its top in an ancient eruption and shattered at least 2,000 feet off its summit. Some volcanic action has continued until recently. Mt. St. Helens probably erupted last in 1840. In this eruption trees were partly buried, died and rotted away, leaving strange "tree holes" in the lava. Steam still emerges from vents in the crater of Mt. Rainier, showing that some of the ancient fire still remains.

Still more great forces were to work on the land we now call Washington. The climate grew cooler all around the world, snows fell and did not melt. These snows packed into ice and grew to great thickness; as they became heavier, they pushed themselves far to the warmer regions of the south; then the weather warmed and they receded. This occurred four times over millions of years, and much of what is northern Washington was covered by ice perhaps thousands of feet thick.

As the crushing masses of ice progressed they brought sand and gravel or rich soil to deposit where they melted. Sometimes they scooped out great troughs or valleys in the earth. Some of these became lakes, such as Chelan. Puget Sound was entirely dry during the period of glaciers. Then as the glaciers melted, the water level rose, and what had been a valley became an inland sea.

The melting water had other tremendous effects. Rivers became mammoth raging torrents, sometimes carving out deep new beds. When some rivers again changed their courses, these deep riverbeds became dry channels called coulees. The melting glaciers caused the "ancestral Columbia" River to become what may have been the mightiest river in the world's history, sometimes called the "grandfather of all rivers." A natural dam of ice where Grand Coulee Dam is today caused the wild, spectacular waters of the ancestral Columbia to cut a new course, a thousand feet deep and fifty miles long, which we know today as the Grand Coulee. The mighty flood thundered over a cliff four hundred feet high and three miles long forming the most stupendous waterfall on earth. When the ice dam melted, the Columbia went back to its old course, and the cliff is now called Dry Falls.

As the glaciers melted, much of central and eastern Washington was covered with a vast ancient lake, called Lake Lewis, and other lakes that exist no longer.

By the time the last glaciers had melted, the land was left much as we know it today.

Every Variation Possible

That land was described by George Vancouver, an early explorer. "The serenity of the climate, the innumerable pleasing landscapes, and the abundant fertility that unassisted nature puts forth, require only to be enriched by the industry of man with villages, mansions, cottages and other buildings to render it the most lovely country that can be imagined."

Vancouver could not have known that on the other side of these lovely valleys and mountains was a land entirely different. What is the state of Washington today might be described as having a split personality. Because the Cascade Mountains keep most of the rainfall on the western slopes, eastern Washington is a dry and sometimes even arid land quite different from the verdant lands of Puget Sound, and yet a land with its own charm and tremendous resources.

Scientists formally divide Washington into seven physiographic areas, that is, areas that are named for the nature of the earth's surface in each area: the Blue Mountains, Columbia Basin, Okanogan Highlands, Cascade Mountains, Puget Sound Basin, Willapa Hills, and Olympic Mountains. These regions differ so much that Washington has almost every topographic variation in the United States.

The Blue Mountains are among the oldest in North America. They rise to an elevation of about 7,000 feet, which gives them sufficient moisture to maintain a forest covering. Their calm, azure-like appearance makes them a land of beauty.

An interesting fact about the slopes of the Blue Mountains and the Palouse region is that the soil is very deep and rich and geologically quite new. The best theory on how this came about is that dust storms from the arid area of central Washington carried top soil west. The moist soil at the base of these mountains tended to hold it. Soil as deep as forty feet accumulated, and it is geologically not more than 2,000 years old.

On both sides of the Columbia River, the land slopes upward to form the vast Columbia Basin, extending from the Cascades to the Idaho border.

North of the Spokane River and the region where the Columbia makes its "Big Bend" is the Okanogan Highlands area—low, gently sloping hills, with park-like meadows and clusters of trees. To the east, the Selkirk Mountains, part of the Rockies, barely touch the northeast corner of Washington.

Most striking natural feature of Washington is the soaring ridge

16

which divides the state fairly evenly into two halves—the Cascade Mountain range. Mt. Rainier, monarch of the range, called the "inspirational landmark of the Northwest," is the highest peak, at 14,410 feet. Mt. St. Helens is often called the "Fujiyama of the western hemisphere" because of its symmetrical form. Rainier, St. Helens, and the other three volcanic mountains are almost entirely different from the neighboring, lower mountains of the range. Mt. Shuksan is said to be one of the oldest mountains in the United States.

The drowned valley of Puget Sound is dotted with the tops of hills, plateaus and mountains that were too high to be covered with water. These became the 300 islands of the Sound. Whidbey Island is the largest, and the group of 172 habitable islands known as the San Juans are the tops of low mountains rising out of this arm of the sea.

The Olympic Mountains are a part of the extensive Coast Range. Tallest of these, Mt. Olympus, is only 7,965 feet high, but because the Olympics rise so abruptly from sea level, their height from base to summit is much greater than many other mountain ranges that rise to higher elevations from lofty plateaus.

South of the Olympics, the Willapa Hills region has heights of less than 3,000 feet, with the steepest slopes found along the bank of the Columbia River.

Washington is the smallest of all the states west of Iowa. However, Washington is only small by comparison, being as large as all of New England, with Delaware thrown in.

Waters—Flowing, Resting and Frozen

Only two rivers flowing through Washington are listed by the United States Geological Survey as major rivers. These are the Columbia and the Snake.

The mighty Columbia has a more even flow of water than any other river in the United States (due to the fact that its tributaries crest at different times), and the greatest flow of any western river—discharging five times the volume of the Colorado River. Only the Columbia has been able to cut through the tough Cascade Mountains, and it also

17

neatly slices the Coast Range. Tides of the Pacific sweep up its lower reaches for 150 miles. It flows across or borders Washington for 750 of its 1,210 miles and drains all of the eastern part of the state.

The Snake is the largest tributary of the Columbia, but only a relatively small part of this unique river flows through Washington. Additional important rivers are the Pend Oreille, Spokane, Yakima, and Skagit. Other Washington rivers, including some of the most interesting names of geography, many of them of Indian origin, are Hamma Hamma, Dosewallips, Duckabush, Soleduck, Hoquiam, Puyallup, Wenatchee, Cedar, Satsop, Wyooche, Chehalis, Okanogan, Duwamish, Nisqually, Pilchuk, Stillaguamish, Snohomish, Deschutes, Nooksack, and Skookumchuck. Numerous spectacular waterfalls include Snoqualmie Falls, Palouse Falls, and Spokane Falls.

Largest natural lake in Washington is glacier-gouged Chelan. Also the deepest, its clear cold waters extend 1,500 feet below the surface in some areas. Franklin D. Roosevelt Lake is backed up almost to the Canadian border by Grand Coulee Dam. Other lakes and reservoirs include famed Lake Washington, 200 feet deep, Soap Lake, Diamond Lake, Silver Lake, Banks Lake, Potholes Reservoir, Omak Lake, Kechelus Lake, Kaches Lake, Cle Elum Lake, Ross Lake, Baker Lake, and Shannon Lake.

One of the most interesting lakes is a lake on a mountain on an island. This is Cascade Lake on Orcas Island. Soap Lake takes its name from the sudsy froth that blows onto shore in a heavy wind. Medical Lake near Spokane is mildly salty.

Eighty per cent of the glacier ice in the United States outside of Alaska is found in Washington. Emmons Glacier on Mt. Rainier is the largest glacier in the United States outside of Alaska. Twenty-six glaciers stretch their icy fingers down the slopes of Mt. Rainier. Twelve major glaciers blanket Mt. Baker, and fifty-three glaciers "inch their way down the slopes of the Olympic range."

At their lowest edges, called terminals, most of the melting water of these glaciers form rivers or creeks. For example, the Nisqually River issues from a spectacular ice cave in Nisqually Glacier on Mt. Rainier. Some of the glaciers are known as "inter glaciers." These are generally lower, and large parts of them melt during the summer season.

However, it is thought that almost all glaciers are growing smaller at a rather rapid rate. As recently as 1885, Nisqually Glacier is thought to have been 1,500 feet longer than it now is.

Other Natural Features

Beacon Rock, near Skamania, is the second largest single rock (monolith) in the world. It rises sheer for 900 feet from the edge of the Columbia River. Only Gibraltar is higher. All along the ocean shore, wind, sea and sand have engraved fantastic carvings on the seaside rocks. Long Beach is said to be the longest hard sand beach in the world. It stretches for twenty miles north of the mouth of the Columbia. Another sandy area of great contrast is the barren desert region of central Washington, where shifting sand dunes murmur as the wind blows their particles.

Memorable gorges and canyons are scattered about the state. Most notable, of course, is the awesome gash cut through the Cascades by the Columbia River. A peculiar and eerie chasm is Z Canyon, only eighteen feet wide and 400 feet deep in places. From the bottom, stars are clearly visible in midday. Other canyons include Green River Gorge near Auburn; Spokane River Canyon near the river's junction with the Columbia; Snake River Canyon, not as stupendous as its up-river Grand Canyon, but still 2,000 feet deep; Grand Canyon of the Grand Ronde River; picturesque Pine Canyon near Waterville; and the canyon of the Klickitat River, where it flows through walls a thousand feet high.

Ice Cave is one of the strange bubble caves in the region south of Mt. Adams, formed when great air bubbles puffed up molten lava and left it to harden into rocky bubbles. Geologists have puzzled long concerning the origin of the "Hole in the Ground" near Spokane, an oasis of natural green, sunk in the desert floor. Equally mysterious are the strange mounds near Tenino. These are symmetrical bumps scattered over the prairie. Dozens of explanations have been given, but no one is at all sure how they came into being.

Interesting in the geography of Washington is the unusual location of Point Roberts. This is the tip of a peninsula extending from the British Columbia coast. Because the peninsula's tip extends south of the 49th parallel, Point Roberts lies in the United States. In order for residents of Point Roberts to reach any other part of the United States by land, they must go through part of Canada.

Climate

The division of the state into two distinct climates is caused by the Cascade Range.

Cool summers and mild winters are the rule in western Washington. Temperatures seldom reach ninety degrees. The slopes of the Olympics have the second greatest rainfall in the United States—145 inches per year, but Seattle averages only about 32 inches annually. Most of the rain comes during the winter. Heavy snows fall only in the mountains. Mt. Rainier had eighty-three feet of snow during one winter, which explains the presence of glaciers.

Eastern Washington has a greater range of temperature, although not extreme either summer or winter. Greatest contrast is in the amount of precipitation, averaging as low as eight inches per year in some regions. In winters much of the eastern section experiences a unique weather phenomenon—the coming of westerly winds called Chinooks. Frosty snow may cover the ground; the aurora borealis flashes at night. Suddenly with a moaning, sighing sound the Chinook comes. The snow begins to melt as if lashed with a blowtorch. Then, as suddenly as it comes, the Chinook may go with the shifting of the wind.

Another weather novelty, especially unusual in dry areas, is the will-o-the-wisp. These are dim, flickering lights often seen darting over the Horse Heaven Hills. Residents of the area also claim to have seen "balls of fire" dashing over the surface with the speed of a car.

Collecting Your Thoughts

Are natural forces still changing the land of Washington?

Is it possible that the land might change as much during future millions of years as it has in the past?

Volcanoes are still being formed from time to time in other parts of the world. Find out more about how mountains such as Rainier may have been created.

Why do many authorities think that present-day glaciers are receding?

Footsteps on the Land

Original and Aboriginal

Remnants of prehistoric people are found in both eastern and western Washington, particularly in the Yakima Valley and Puget Sound regions. If people have lived in Washington as long as they apparently have in other western regions, they have occupied the area for 20,000, perhaps even 30,000 years.

Many of the picture writings (pictographs) and carvings (petroglyphs) found on rocks and canyons in Washington are thought to have been made by ancient peoples. Pictographs near Buffalo Rock showing men with wide square shoulders, squat legs, and headdresses with horns are considered to be the work of people about 3,000 years ago known as Basketmakers. A petroglyph near Rogersburg shows two men in mortal combat with flint knives. Petroglyphs above Rock Island Dam have either been covered by the water or barely show above it, but there are many other works of prehistoric art in the state.

Carved stone images have been found in The Dalles region; some of these represented the heads of monkeys, but nothing more is known about them.

In late historic times the Indians of what is now Washington have been divided into two groups known as the Horse Indians and Canoe Indians. The two groups had distinctly different habits and customs. This came about because of the two different types of climate to the east and the west of the Cascade Range. The Horse Indians were nomads, moving about as the hunting and weather varied, living in portable lodges carried about from one campsite to another. The Canoe Indians lived in winter in permanent dwellings, cedar-planked, called longhouses and in temporary lodges in summer.

Some of the coastal lodges were enormous, and many related families lived in them. The Old-Man-House of the Suquamish Indians may have covered an acre and a quarter. Inside there were forty apartments divided by split logs. Coastal Indians were noted for their canoe making. Sometimes canoes sixty-feet long would be carved from a single cedar log, the inside hollowed out by red hot stones and stone axes and the outside carefully smoothed with expert care. The canoes were so skillfully designed that they were noted for seaworthiness. Dogfish liver oil, rubbed on in many coats, was used to preserve the hulls. Although this made a frightful odor, its preservative qualities have kept canoes in floating condition for more than a hundred years.

In other crafts, especially woodcarving, the coast Indians of Washington were not as skillful as their cousins to the north in British Columbia and Alaska. Until modern times there was no genuine totem art in what is now Washington. In recent years Washington Indians have been taught how to carve totems by Alaskan natives. The Makah Indians were more nearly like the Alaskan Indians in customs, crafts and whaling. Most Washington coastal Indians had skill in basket-making, dyeing, bead work, and making of rather crude dog-hair blankets. They did not use feathers for headdresses or decorations.

Coast Indians had three distinct classes—the nobility, middle class, and slaves; women held a distinctly inferior place. There were heredi-tary chiefs and medicine men, called shamans, who often became rich and powerful. The people believed that spirits were everywhere and that each person had his own guardian spirit. A shaman would preside at the spirit dances when young people obtained their guardian spirits. They also administered to the sick, and often lost their lives when the cures failed to work.

The Indians had a host of interesting legends. One of the most unusual of these concerns the origin of Sol Duc Hot Springs on the Olympic Peninsula. According to the story, two mighty, fiery dragons, Elwha and Sol Duc, fought a terrible battle. When neither of them could win, they each slunk back to their caves and wept hot tears, which have been draining down ever since to form the springs.

The coastal Indians were rather mild and not especially warlike; they suffered greatly when raiding Haida tribesmen swept down from the north to conquer Washington Indians for slaves.

There was little visiting between interior Indians and coastal Indians. Sometimes Klickitat Indians from the Columbia River, riding their sturdy ponies, went to visit their Puget Sound cousins. Infrequently the coastal Indians returned the visit to pick nuts and berries. The Klickitat tribe possessed hereditary rights of fishing at Celilo Falls. They dried much salmon into pemican and bartered this with many other tribes.

23

CELILO FALLS

These ancient fishing treaty rights were held until the famous falls disappeared under the waters of a man-made lake.

One of the strangest burial grounds in the country was Memaloose Island (Place of the Dead) where burial canoes were placed high in trees of the island. The wealth of the dead was placed beside them in their canoes where they waited for the "flood of life."

The Horse Indians received this title because of the importance of horses in their way of life. Soon after horses were reintroduced to the American continent by the Spaniards, the Indians east of the Cascades began to breed their own types of ponies. The Nez Perce were noted for their beautiful and unique spotted appaloosa ponies, one of the truly distinct and remarkable breeds of horses. Horse Indians depended greatly on roots for food, and they were skilled in basketry and leather tanning. They were fond of feathered ornaments of all kinds.

Horse Indians also had their chiefs, shamans and spirits; the Spokane Indians felt they had a particular association with the sun.

Many Indian terms have been taken into the English language; two of these are tillicum (friend) and potlach. Both Horse and Canoe Indians held potlaches. These were parties at which everyone tried to outdo his neighbor in the lavish gifts given. Then those who were entertained were expected to give a potlach and attempt to provide even more lavish presents. Some wealthy Indians died in poverty because of their extravagant potlaches.

Another peculiar custom of the coast Indians was "cradling." Heads of Indian babies were bound to cradle boards to flatten them for greater "beauty." In the springtime, uncradling ceremonies were held, and the boards and binding were hidden away in holes or caves to keep away evil spirits.

Tribal and family groups were much smaller among the Canoe Indians, and there were many group names associated with them, including Suquamish, Duwamish, Snoqualmie, Squally, Puyallup, Cowlitz, Nisqually, Nooksack, Lummi, Wahkiakum, Cathlamet, and Makah. Principal Horse Indian tribes included the Yakima, Walla Walla, Cayuse, Spokane and the famed Nez Perce. Altogether there were about thirty-six main tribal groups in the region now called Washington.

White Sails in the Sunset

In 1592, just a hundred years after Columbus discovered America, Apostolos Valerianos, a Greek who sailed for the Spaniards under the name of Juan de Fuca, is said to have discovered the strait which bears his name. Today this is believed to be little more than a myth.

Almost another two-hundred years were to pass before discovery of the region now known as Washington was actually recorded. In 1774 Juan Perez sailed along the coast and saw a mountain which he named Santa Rosalia (now Olympus). A year later Bruno Heceta and Juan de Bodega y Quadra stepped ashore on the Olympic Coast near Point Grenville and became the first Europeans known to have touched what is now Washington. They took possession of the region in the name of the king of Spain. They probably saw the mouth of the Columbia River, but did not recognize it as the long-sought "river of the West."

Renowned English explorer, Captain James Cook, named Cape Flattery in 1778, but for some strange reason missed the strait just "around the corner." In the same year Captain James Meares named Mount Olympus, because the original Mount Olympus in Greece was the mythical home of the gods, and he felt this Olympus was also fit for the gods.

Nine years passed before Captain Charles William Barkley discovered what we now call the Strait of Juan de Fuca and gave it that name to honor the man who may have seen it first. In 1790 a Spanish force under Francisco Eliza took possession of Neah Bay, and one of the members of the company, Manual Quimper, explored the San Juan Islands and sighted Mount Baker but missed Puget Sound. The Spaniards brought the first settlers to Washington and established a settlement at Neah Bay, but it was abandoned within five months.

One spring morning Chief Kitsap, leader of many tribes, stood on the shore with his people and watched a huge white bird approach their shores. To these believers in many spirits, this must have seemed to be the approach of the Great Spirit. Actually this was the ship of English Captain George Vancouver making his historic discovery of Puget Sound in 1792. He gave it a thorough exploration and named it for his friend and lieutenant, Peter Puget.

In that same year Captain Robert Gray of the United States conducted his second voyage to the region and made what later proved to be the most important discovery of all—the long-sought river to the interior. He braved the almost impossible currents and entered the great broad mouth of the river which he named for his ship, the *Columbia*. On May 12, he landed near the place now called Fort Columbia. Thousands of Indians from nearby villages came to watch in awed silence as this mammoth winged canoe discharged its pale strangers.

Vancouver and Gray had given both England and the United States strong claim to the region, and the stage was set for the development of what has come to be known as the Northwest or Oregon Country.

"Unequaled in American History"

The most notable exploration of the West and one of our greatest sources of national pride was the expedition of Lewis and Clark, sent by President Jefferson to learn about the countryside and prepare the Indians for the coming of Americans. In October, 1805, after a journey including almost every known peril and hardship, the party reached the mouth of the Clearwater River where it joins the Snake at what is now the eastern boundary of Washington. They are credited with discovering the Snake.

At about that point Captain Clark wrote: *". . . our diet extremely bad nothing but roots and dried fish to eate, all the Party have greatly the advantage of me, in as much as they all relish the flesh of the dogs, Several of which we purchased of the native. . . . The Pierced nose Indians (Nez Perce) are Stout likely men, handsom women, and verry dressey in their way, the dress of the men are a White Buffalow robe or Elk Skin dressed with Beeds which are generally white, Sea Shells and the Mother of Pirl hung to their hair . . . feathers, and different coloured Paints which they find in their country. . . . The women dress in a shirt of Ibex or Goat Skins which reach quite down to their anckles. . . ."*

Lewis and Clark and their men moved on down the Snake past rapids and canyons to the Columbia. Several times their canoes upset and precious supplies were lost or soaked. They saw more and more Indians fishing for salmon and the party became very tired of their salmon diet. On October 19, Clark wrote, *"I descovered a high mountain of emence hight covered with Snow, this must be one of the mountains laid down by Vancouver, as seen from the mouth of the Columbia River."* Scholars think probably this was Mt. Adams. They continued over dangerous rapids, portaged around Celilo Falls and then reached The Dalles. Clark wrote, *"The whole Current of this great river must at all Stages pass thro' this narrow chanel of 45 yards wide. . . . I deturmined to pass through this place notwithstanding the horrid appearance of this agitated swelling boiling and whorling in every direction . . . however we passed Safe to the astonishment of all the Inds. of the last lodges who viewed us from the top of the rock."*

Finally they whirled over the fierce Cascades of the Columbia to *"proceed on down a smoth gentle Stream of about 2 miles wide, in which the tide has its effect as high as . . . the Last rapids at Strawberry Islands."* Further on, at last after crossing the continent Clark was able to report, *"Great joy in camp we are in view of the Ocian, this great Pacific Octean which we been so long anxious to see. and the roreing or noise made by the waves . . . may be heard distinctly."*

For a time they stayed on the Washington side of the Columbia, where Captain Clark carved his famous words on a pine tree: "William Clark December 3rd 1805. By Land from the U. States in 1804 & 1805." The party spent the winter on the Oregon side of the Columbia and started back on Sunday, March 23, 1806, trading with the Indians and treating their ailments as they went. In May they passed out of what is now Washington on their homeward trip.

Their management of the Indians and winning their friendship was one of their greatest accomplishments. Lewis and Clark liked the Indians, and Clark had special skills in dealing with them. The proud Nez Perce remained friendly for over sixty years because of the admiration for Americans gained through Lewis and Clark and their strong and faithful men.

Furs and Fortresses

The reports of Lewis and Clark fired the imagination of their country-men and gave them the first indication that one day the Stars and Stripes might fly "from sea to shining sea."

Inspired by Lewis and Clark's detailed accounts of the large number of fur-bearing animals in the region, American businessman, John Jacob Astor, in 1811 sent men to establish the first settlement, Fort Astoria, in the Oregon country, just across the Columbia from present-day Washington. Indians brought their furs to Astoria in exchange for manufactured goods. Wilson Price Hunt brought the second party ever to make its way overland across the United States.

British David Thompson arrived at the mouth of the Columbia just after construction of Astoria had started. He had been surveying and setting up fur-trading posts clear across lower Canada. In 1810 he had already established Spokane House, the first fur-trading post in the region. This was at the junction of the Spokane and Little Spokane rivers. Two years later the Astor company set up its own trading house, Fort Spokane, not far away.

In 1811 David Stuart of the Astor party had established Fort Okanogan on the Okanogan River, the first settlement within the present boundaries of Washington to fly the American flag.

During the War of 1812, John Jacob Astor transferred his Astoria properties to the great Canadian fur organization, the North West

FORT VANCOUVER

Company. The North West Company established Fort Walla Walla in 1818. Later that company and the mammoth British Hudson's Bay Company were combined, and the Hudson's Bay Company took over the trading posts on the Columbia and its tributaries. The company abandoned Spokane House in 1821 and moved company headquarters from Astoria to a new location which they called Fort Vancouver on the banks of the Columbia. This was the first permanent settlement in what is now Washington.

King of the Columbia

Chosen to build Fort Vancouver and to be Chief Factor, leader, in the whole region of the Columbia was Dr. John McLoughlin, a little-known figure in American history but one of the most remarkable. Although only forty-one years old, the doctor had snow-white hair hanging to his shoulders and stood straight as an arrow, well over six-feet tall. His appearance was so impressive that the Indians regarded him with awe, and no one ever controlled the Indians so justly or so well.

He worked closely with powerful one-eyed Chief Comcomly of the Chinook, and they became very friendly. With the help of such native leaders, Dr. McLoughlin kept peace in the whole vast region under his control throughout the twenty-two years he served as almost a king of a land far larger than that controlled by many real kings.

By 1828, only four years after Fort Vancouver was founded, Dr. John and his men had built a civilization in the wilderness. Famed American fur trader and merchant, Jedediah Smith, visited Fort Vancouver that year and wrote, *"The crop of 1828 was 700 bu. of wheat, fourteen acres of corn, the same of peas . . . about 200 head of cattle, 52 horses, 300 head of hogs. . . . They have mechanics, coopers, blacksmiths, gunsmiths, carpenters, tinners and a good saw mill . . . a grist mill. . . . Their influence on the Indians is now decisive."* For twenty-five years Fort Vancouver was known as "the most populous settlement in half a continent."

As the years went by, the company of the fort lived in great style. Whenever Dr. McLoughlin or any important visitor arrived or left the fort the official piper in his dress kilts piped them on their way. With

PLANT THEM IN
YOUR STRANGE LAND

his pipes he was always behind Dr. McLoughlin's chair at the banquet table.

Eva E. Dye in her book "McLoughlin and Old Oregon" described the life there: "The fort dining hall was a noble apartment capable of seating 500 guests. A huge map of the Indian country covered the wall. The dinner bell rang and the long tables began to fill. With a wave of the hand the stately governor seated his guests according to rank. Before them cut-glass and silver with the McLoughlin coat of arms, shone side by side with modern queen's ware and rare old china. Dr. McLoughlin presided like a picture out of the old colonial time, clean-shaven, fair and rosy, with his white locks twisted into a queue at the back. . . . The fire-logs flickered in the dark old chimney, and the branching candelabra sent out an odor of perfumed wax."—an amazing picture of accomplishment by people surrounded by hundreds of miles of wilderness.

The same author tells how the very first apples came to what became the world's greatest apple country: "The fruitful orchard at Fort Vancouver had sprung from a handful of seeds dropped into the pocket of an old ship-captain by a laughing girl across the sea. 'Take them and plant them in your savage land,' she said. The black satin vest was packed away in a sea-chest. In airing his clothes one day at Fort Vancouver the seeds fell out. 'Bless me! bless me! let us start an orchard,' said Dr. McLoughlin, picking up the little triangular treasures. Another sea captain brought a bunch of peach-stones from Crusoe's Island Juan Fernandez. A little planting, a little care, peaches."

The fur-trading empire ruled by Dr. McLoughlin had grown rapidly. His men ruled outposts on Puget Sound at present-day Dupont, on the middle Columbia, at Fort Walla Walla, the upper Columbia, Fort Colville at Kettle Falls, and even as far away as present Idaho. To these and other posts came Indians with rich beaver and other furs to trade for blankets, pots and pans, and many ornamental or useful products that only the white man could provide. The Indians would have traded everything they had for rum but Dr. McLoughlin had strict rules that this should never be done. He knew it brought most Indians to complete ruin. He did everything he could to prevent "Yankee" traders from bringing rum to the Indians.

Wagons West!

Although Dr. McLoughlin was a ruler in fact, he was not a ruler in title. Both Britain and the United States claimed what came to be known as the Oregon Country—Oregon, Washington, parts of Idaho, and some other areas with boundaries not very well defined. In 1818 both nations had agreed that each would have equal rights in the region for a period of ten years. In 1827 that joint occupancy was continued indefinitely. The Hudson's Bay Company remained supreme for so long only because of its great wealth and power and the business genius of Dr. McLoughlin in keeping other traders out.

However, a small independent settlement was set up in the Willamette Valley in what is now Oregon, and a few Americans drifted into the region. Then in 1843 the first large group of settlers came overland from the United States by covered wagon, establishing the famed Oregon Trail. Over this trail in the next few years moved an incredible number of people, mostly settling south of the Columbia.

Britain hoped to keep the region north of the Columbia, but the American people had been aroused. They elected James K. Polk President on a slogan of "54-40 or Fight." This meant that the people would accept nothing less than a boundary between the United States and Canada placed above the 54th parallel. For a time a war seemed likely over this quarrel, but in 1846 a compromise was made (aided by the fact of the settlement at Tumwater) that continued the boundary along the 49th parallel to the coast, giving Canada all of Vancouver Island.

The largest section of the old Oregon Territory, including Washington, had become a part of the United States. Dr. McLoughlin resigned and moved to Oregon, and the power of the Hudson's Bay Company grew less.

Martyrs at Waiilatpu

In 1836 a remarkable man came into Dr. McLoughlin's domain. This was Dr. Marcus Whitman. Both he and Dr. McLoughlin were medical doctors who had entered other fields. Dr. Whitman had become a Presbyterian missionary. On September 16, 1836, Dr. Whitman and the Rev. Henry H. Spalding arrived at Fort Vancouver and were greeted by Dr. McLoughlin. With the missionaries were their recent brides, Narcissa and Eliza. They had just become the first white women to make the complete overland journey from coast to coast by wagon, horseback and boat.

Dr. McLoughlin approved the noble purpose of the missionaries but he feared the difficulties he knew they faced. After a day or two of rest, Spalding and Whitman left to find spots for two missions. Henry Spalding chose a spot in present Idaho.

Whitman selected a location among the decadant Cayuse Indians, not far from Walla Walla. He called the mission Waiilatpu, the "Place of the Rye Grass." He taught the Indians much about farming and other ways of life, but was never very successful in converting them to Christianity. Another mission was founded in 1838 in the Spokane country by Cushing Eels, Elkanah Walker, and their wives. They had little success either. Eels wrote, "We have been here almost nine years and have not yet been permitted to hear the cry of one penitent or the song of one redeemed soul."

That same year Father Francois Norbert founded St. Francis Mission near present Mary's Corner, the first Roman Catholic mission in what is now Washington. This is the oldest continuing mission in the state. Fathers Modeste Demers and Francois Blanchet set up another Catholic mission at Cowlitz in 1839.

Dr. Marcus Whitman, a great patriot of the United States, never gave up his determination that all of Oregon Territory should belong to his country. He made a terribly difficult overland trip in winter back to Washington, D. C., to try to persuade government officials to take greater interest in the territory. He was influential in bringing the first large group of settlers over the Oregon Trail.

This patriotism helped in his undoing. Mrs. Whitman wrote to her mother, "The poor Indians are amazed at the overwhelming numbers of Americans coming into the country. They seem not to know what to make of it. Husband is wearing out fast; his heart and hands are so full all the time that his brethren feel solicitous about him. His benevolence is unbounded, and he often goes to the extent of his ability and beyond in doing good to the Indians and white men."

The white immigrants brought measles, deadly to the Indians, and smallpox, even more deadly. Hundreds died; discontent grew. They blamed Dr. Whitman for infecting them with disease. Finally, in 1847, the Cayuse Indians attacked Waiilatpu, murdering Dr. and Mrs. Whitman and eight others. Dr. and Mrs. Spalding and their daughter were not injured at their mission among the Nez Perce.

In the account of Eva Dye, a messenger brought the news of the massacre to Chief Pio-pio-mox-mox, always a friend of the Americans. " 'Doct' Whit'n is killed.'

" 'What part had you in it?' inquired the chief, fixing his Egyptian eye upon the herald. Proud of his exploits, intent only on making them great as possible, the runner said, 'Me? I wounded one, I struck one, and I killed one.'

" 'Take that man and hang him to the nearest tree,' cried Pio-pio-mox-mox, in a tone of thunder.

"The attendants seized the boaster, and before he realized it was not a jest, the noose tightened about his neck. In a few moments a corpse dangled from the boughs of a rugged old cottonwood."

The provisional government of Oregon which had been set up by the settlers borrowed money to make war on the Indians, and they were successful in this Cayuse War. Several of the Indian massacre party later were tried and hanged.

Oregon Territory

In 1848 Congress passed a bill forming Oregon Territory. This included all of Oregon and Washington and portions of Idaho. A young man who was then not very well known but who showed great promise was offered the governorship but he refused to take it. His name was Abraham Lincoln. The choice for first governor then fell to General Joseph Lane, and he reached Oregon City in March, 1849.

Settlement was encouraged when Congress passed the Donation Land Claim Act in 1850. This provided means for settlers to claim the land.

Developments came rapidly; the Oregon Trail was blazed through to the Puget Sound region; by 1851 Olympia was a thriving village at the southern end of the Sound. In that year it became the first port of entry on the Sound with a customs house. Steilacoom had become a bustling seaport, with Fort Steilacoom established only a mile away.

In 1851 an even more notable settlement took place. A small group of settlers arrived at Portland and sent two of their group ahead to the Puget Sound area to locate the best spot for a town. They began to build a cabin on the south headland of what is now Elliott Bay and wrote to the others at Portland, "Come as soon as you can; we have found a valley that will support thousands of families." This was an interesting and modest prediction.

The others came, about two dozen who had made the long trip overland from the East, arriving in Elliott Bay on the schooner *Exact*. They gave their settlement the name New York, adding the Indian word "Alki," meaning "bye and bye." One of them described their new land:

"an incomparable harbor, vast tracts of timber, salmon-filled waters, good farmland, benign climate." There seemed to be everything needed for a good life.

When they found that the shallow sandy beach of Alki Point was not a suitable spot for a timber port, some of them took Mary Denny's clothesline and went searching for a deep water harbor, testing the depth with a horseshoe to weight the clothesline. They found the perfect spot and moved their settlement to the site where Seattle grew and so it might be said that the greatest metropolis of the Northwest owes its location to a clothesline.

One of the early businessmen, Dr. David S. Maynard, wanted to give the new community the name of a friendly chief of the Duwamish, Suquamish, and other Indian groups. The chief was afraid that this might offend his guardian spirit, but at last he consented and the future city took the name of Seattle, a much admired chief.

Settlement of what is now Washington grew so rapidly and development came so quickly that by 1853 Congress passed and President Millard Fillmore signed a bill creating Washington Territory. Some had wanted the name to be Columbia, but to others it seemed proper that the future state should bear the name of the first President. Senator Stephen A. Douglas wanted to call the territory Washingtonia, to distinguish it from the nation's Capital but that was defeated. Isaac Ingalls Stevens was elected first Governor of Washington Territory, which included what is now northern Idaho and western Montana.

Collecting Your Thoughts

Read more about the Indian custom of potlaches.

Lewis and Clark and their men kept many interesting daily diaries and journals of the trip. After reading more on the subject, write an account of a day's journey in what is now Washington as though you were a member of the party.

In what ways was the work of Dr. John McLoughlin important in development of Washington? List as many as possible.

The early settlers of Seattle had many interesting experiences with the Indians; read about these and select the most interesting.

Yesterday and Today

To Save Their Ancestral Homes

The Indians were thoroughly alarmed at the flood of immigrants settling on their ancestral lands. They organized to make war and drive off the invaders. Governor Stevens met the Canoe Indian tribes of Nisqually, Puyallup, and Squaxon at Medicine Creek and made a treaty with them in 1854. This was the first of many treaties in which the Indians agreed to accept reservations.

Then he went east in 1855 to a great council of 6,000 Horse Indians where the city of Walla Walla now stands. The Nez Perce alone had almost 2,000 tribesmen there. During the meeting, 3,000 Indian horses grazed calmly on the pastures around the meeting place. The great Chief Joseph, Chiefs Lawyer and Timothy of the Nez Perce, Pio-pio-mox-mox of the Walla Walla, Kamiakin and Ow-hi of the Yakima, and many other leaders represented their people.

Governor Stevens urged them to take reservation lands where they would have the advantages of government schools, mills, stores and scientific agriculture. The Indians thought the lands offered them were poor and small; at one time a massacre of Stevens and his aides was prevented only by the help of Chief Lawyer. At last, however, the majority agreed to sign a treaty accepting reservations. At this point Chief Looking Glass arrived and lamented, "My people, what have you done? While I was gone you have sold my country. I have come home, and there is not left for me a place on which to pitch my lodge."

Indian leaders and tribes on both sides of the Cascades disowned or disregarded the treaties, and there was fairly general Indian war throughout the Washington Territory from 1855 through 1858. Eastern Washington was closed to miners and settlers in 1855.

The Klickitat Indians attacked the village of Seattle in 1856. The United States sloop-of-war *Decatur* arrived in Elliott Harbor just in time to help defeat the Indians and save Seattle. The *Decatur* had gone aground near Port Blakely and had barely managed to reach Seattle.

Eastern tribes and chiefs provided more resistance than the Canoe tribes, many of which remained neutral. Major Granville O. Haller had been defeated in the Simcoe Mountains. But Yakima Chief Kamiakin suffered a severe defeat in 1856. In 1858, Lieutenant-Colonel Edward J. Steptoe was attacked by Palouse Indians in what has been called the Battle of Rosalia. After suffering several casualties he and most of his men were able to escape in darkness.

After this battle, 700 soldiers under Colonel George Wright met 5,000 Indians in the Battle of Four Lakes in August, 1858. Because of their superior weapons the small white force won a victory over the much larger army. On September 5, 1858, Wright defeated the Indians decisively at the Battle of Spokane Plains. Shortly afterward Colonel Wright rounded up a herd of 700 Indian horses, which he had shot in order to "ground" the Indians and keep them from carrying on the war. For many years the bone pile from this slaughter was used for fertilizer. Even now occasional bones may be found from these animal casualties of war.

Many tragedies occurred on both sides. Settlers and other innocent victims were massacred, and great injustices were perpetrated on many individual Indians as well. Chief Quiemuth of the Nisqually surrendered and was murdered by a settler. Another Nisqually leader, Chief Leschi, also surrendered and was "hanged on perjured testimony."

At last most of the Indian troubles came to an end in 1858 as the Indians began to see that they could not overcome the flood of settlers descending on their land. Chief Seattle, who had not taken part in the wars, made a pathetic but memorable prediction, "When the last red man shall have perished and the memory of my tribe shall have become a myth among the white men, these shores will swarm with the invisible dead of my tribe. . . . At night when the streets of your cities and villages are silent and you think them deserted, they will throng with the returning hosts that once filled them and still love this beautiful land. The white man will never be alone."

The Pig War

Both England and the United States claimed the San Juan Islands, and ownership had never been decided definitely. English and American settlers occupied parts of the islands. Both sides tried to collect customs and taxes. There was constant tension in the area.

In 1859 a pig owned by English Charles J. Griffin got into a vegetable garden of American Lyman A. Cutler. Cutler immediately shot the pig and said he would do the same to any British authority who tried to interfere. The British demanded that Cutler be brought to trial, and the United States sent troops into the area under Captain George Pickett, later to become famous for his fantastic "charge" at the Battle of Gettysburg. The British then sent their own troops. Fortunately, no fighting occurred in this "Pig War," and finally the troops became so friendly they tried to outdo each other in lavish parties given in a kind of imitation of the native potlaches.

Later both sides accepted Emperor Wilhelm I of Germany as an arbiter to decide the ownership, and he awarded the San Juan Islands to the United States in 1872. Because it was such a colorful and unique event, newspapers refer to the Pig War frequently. The National Parks Bureau has plans for further commemoration of the event.

Change and Growth

When Oregon became a state in 1859, the parts of Oregon Territory not included in the new state were added to Washington Territory, enlarging the boundaries considerably.

During this period the demand for lumber and the huge supplies of timber and the discovery of gold in various parts of the territory or adjoining lands were the greatest causes for growth of population and economic development. One of the first gold rushes occurred near Old Fort Colville. Gold mining began at Wenatchee in 1858 and gold was worked in the Similkameen River in 1859. Bellingham was the best access point to the scene of a gold rush on the Fraser River in Canada, and the population of Bellingham rose to 15,000, although it soon dropped again. In the early sixties, deposits were worked in the Sultan Basin, Snohomish County, in Whatcom County at Ruby Creek, in the Peshastin Creek district near Blewett, and Swauk country near Mt. Stuart.

Washington was too remote and too little populated to be much concerned with the Civil War when it came in 1861. However, many residents remembered several military men who had served in Washington and had become famous in the war, including Generals Pickett, Grant, Sherman, and Sheridan—almost a who's who of the Civil War. Former Washington Territory Governor Stevens was killed in the Battle of Chantilly.

In 1861 eastern residents tried to pass a bill dividing Washington at the Cascades, but the legislature defeated this. In 1863 Congress created Idaho Territory, leaving Washington with today's boundaries except for the San Juans.

Coming of the 1870's brought the first climbing of Mount Rainier by P. B. Van Trump and General Hazard Stevens on August 17, 1870. More important in the progress of the territory was the first permanent settlement of Spokane, then known as Spokane Falls, in 1871. Ten years later, on the Northern Pacific, the first train puffed into that small but energetic settlement and brought with it rapid advancement. The Spokane Falls *Review* reported enthusiastically, "New dwellings, new stores, and new manufacturing establishments are springing up like magic, and the end is not yet."

Railroads meant life or death for many communities, and when established towns were bypassed by a railroad, they often died or faded. When the Northern Pacific decided to go four miles north of the town

of Yakima, the entire town of 100 buildings was put on skids and rollers and trundled out to the railroad line. Hotels, bars, and stores did a thriving business as they went. Finally the Northern Pacific reached Tacoma in 1887 by the use of switchbacks over the Cascades, giving the wealth of the Northwest an outlet to the East.

As in any frontier area many of the aspects of the "wild west" have become a part of Washington's history, along with a few distinctive twists of its own, such as smugglers and fish pirates. The once thriving Okanogan County Seat town of Ruby was noted for its mining stampedes and adventurers of the many types who usually descended on mining communities. Fingers were quick on the trigger, and tough saloons were the center of social life. Ruby was once known as the "Babylon of Washington Territory."

One of the leading Ruby citizens supplied his butcher shop through his cattle rustling activities until cattlemen of the region came to town with a rope. At their insistance, the butcher-rustler was brought to trial but was freed.

The year 1889 brought a strange combination of triumph and disaster. The almost completely wooden cities of Seattle, Spokane, Vancouver and Ellensburg all were swept by terrible fires. Damage in Seattle was fifteen million dollars and wiped out almost the entire business section,

but in the next year alone reconstruction there totalled ten million. The loss at Spokane was six million dollars.

The State of Washington

Triumph came when on November 11, 1889, President Benjamin Harrison proclaimed creation of the new state of Washington, with Elisha P. Ferry as first governor, and with John B. Allen of Walla Walla and Watson B. Squire of Seattle as the first United States Senators from the new state.

The decade of the 1890's saw the beginning of the "apple fever" as semi-arid lands were reclaimed and extensive orchards planted.

The Great Northern arrived at Seattle in 1893, and started a new boom in that city. Another new wave of prosperity came in 1897 when thousands of gold hunters began to use Seattle as the gateway and supply point for the gold fields of the Yukon and Alaska. About the same time, Washington had a small gold rush of its own in the Republic area.

As the old century waned, the tremendous values of the Mt. Rainier region to the nation were recognized when Mt. Rainier National Park was created on March 2, 1899.

In 1902 the first railroad bridge crossed the Columbia River. Seattle, scarcely more than fifty years old, held a great fair in 1909—The Alaska-Yukon-Pacific Exposition, on a site now occupied by the University of Washington. The forward-looking city established in that same year its Metropolitan Center, claimed to be the first planned business district in the United States. The Metropolitan Center is still owned by the University of Washington, and the income from it adds greatly to the financial support of the institution. During the decade of 1900-1910, the population of Washington increased 120 per cent.

The worst railroad disaster in the state's history occurred in 1910. Two trains stalled at Wellington by snows were swept 400 feet into the canyon below by an avalanche which also carried the station with it. One hundred eighteen persons were killed in this tragedy.

In the greater tragedy of World War I, 67,694 men and 632 women from Washington served their country, and of these 1,622 men and three women lost their lives in that conflict. Just after the war, in 1919, Seattle was paralyzed by a five-day general strike, the first ever to be called in the nation.

As Washington moved into the modern age, great changes were taking place. As rich timber areas became logged off, many cities and towns suffered severe setbacks. Some were able to substitute other income producing activities and make a slow comeback; others simply died and became ghosts. The movement toward sustained yield of forests forged ahead.

Coming of the automobile, the bus and the motor truck revolutionized much of the way of life of the area. Automation of farming caused farms, especially in the east, to grow greatly in size and require fewer people to grow larger crops. When those no longer needed on the farms were forced to move to the city, more jobs for them were necessary. Many of these powerful forces are touched on in later sections.

The year 1920 saw the world's first international air-mail service, flown by Edward Hubbard from Seattle to Victoria, British Columbia.

One of the largest projects of the kind carried out in the United States up to its time was the second Cascade tunnel, completed in 1929.

As the financial depression of the thirties moved drearily along, Washington suffered with the rest of the nation. An unusual attempt in Washington to overcome the effects of the depression made national headlines. When a bank failed in Tenino, the town turned to its great natural timber resource and created wooden currency, called "lumberjack." This "money" has now become a collectors' item.

Olympic National Park was created in 1938, and Washington celebrated the Golden Jubilee of its statehood in 1939.

Powerhouse of the Atom

World War II brought to Washington some of the most interesting, important and dramatic happenings away from the battle lines. The largest construction project in the history of the world to that time, Grand Coulee Dam, completed in 1941, had created in Washington one of the world's greatest electric power sources. That power was to be used in a remarkable way.

Richland had been a sleepy village of 250 people. In 1881 Lt. Thomas W. Symons said of the area, "It is a desolation where even the most hopeful can find nothing in its future prospects to cheer."

Almost overnight this became one of the world's worst prophecies. Suddenly 45,000 men were working feverishly on a secret project near Richland, housed in the new Richland—a roaring tar-paper metropolis that sprang up like magic at the command of the federal government.

Here was a key part of one of the world's most carefully kept secrets. Thousands of men in a great manufacturing establishment called the Hanford Plant engaged in mysterious work which only a handful of them understood at all. Not until the atomic bomb was revealed did it become known that people of the Hanford Plant were creating raw material for the most destructive weapon the world had ever known, and also for what might become one of the most important peacetime tools ever developed by mankind. They were using the almost limitless power of Grand Coulee electricity to transmute uranium into plutonium, the basis of atomic power.

In the midst of security brownouts and jitters over possible invasion of the state closest to raging Japan, Washington also carried out other vital war work. The most destructive machines ever built until that time were pouring out of the Boeing airplane plant—B-17 Flying Fortresses and B-29 Super-Fortresses. A constant stream of ships issued from the ways of Washington's great shipyards, everything from enormous aircraft carriers to cargo-convoy ships.

During the war hosts of men and women of Washington served in the armed forces, and tragic numbers lost their lives. Less than ten years later, in 1950, another war, this time in Korea, brought more thousands of Washingtonians into service, and many more were killed.

A New Empire of Many Peoples

One of Nature's worst blows was struck in 1955 when a disastrous freeze killed almost all of Washington's apple trees over eight years old. But this was only a temporary setback for the industry and the booming state.

Seattle's world's fair in 1962 brought a host of visitors into the state.

It was carefully designed to leave, after its close, a heritage of many fine buildings and other facilities. Seattle now enjoys more useful facilities from its fair than was realized from any other fair in history.

The year 1965 brought a severe and damaging earthquake centered north of Seattle and felt over all the state, but this left few permanent marks.

Today, a land that was a wilderness little more than a century ago has become the beloved home of almost three million people. These people include Hawaiians descended from some of the original settlers of the state at Vancouver, Dutch, Finns, Norwegians, Chinese, Japanese, Filipinos, Irish, Italians and people from the Balkans, Croatians, Swiss, Poles, among others. However, one authority writes, "We are still predominately Scandinavian. It is said that a name like 'Anderson' is worth 100,000 votes in any state election."

Of the original settlers of the region—the Indians—there are still 12,000 descendants of forty-five Indian tribes on twenty-one reservations. Although the Indian people proudly maintain the heritage of their culture, they take an active part in modern citizenship. Their many annual festivals form an important part of the tourist attractions of the state. The extent to which these original Americans have become "Americanized" is illustrated by a sign on the wall in the meeting house of the Quinault tribe, which reads "The trouble with this tribe is that there are too many chiefs and not enough Indians."

Working together, the peoples of Washington have fulfilled the prophecy of the pioneers that "cities and villages shall spring up on the west . . . and a new empire shall be added to the kingdoms of the earth."

Collecting Your Thoughts

Name as many as you can of the causes of the Indian wars.

Why were the railroads so important?

Many interesting stories are told about the coming of various ethnic groups, such as the Hawaiians at Vancouver. Choose one of these and get more information about them.

Name as many reasons as you can why the Richland area was chosen for its part in the production of atomic materials.

Natural Treasures

Heavens and Havens

From time to time motorists in the Horse Heaven Hills will see a perky colt prancing close to the road, with his mother anxiously close behind in fear that he may be hurt by the great snorting beasts going along the road. A proud, sleek bay may sometimes make an appearance. These are some of the remnants of once great herds of wild horses supported on the abundant pastures of these hills. The last big roundup of wild horses in Washington took place near Ephrata in 1906.

Gone now is an even more unusual "wild" animal of Washington—the camel. Brought in as mine pack animals, they were unsuitable on rocky ground, and some were turned loose in the Okanogan hills to startle many an unsuspecting stranger.

Almost half a million deer range the state, including black- and white-tailed and mule. The Olympic Mountains are noted for their elk, and other elk herds are found elsewhere in the state, totaling close to 50,000 including the rare Roosevelt elk. Possibly there are more mountain goats in Washington than any other state, an estimated 6,000. Bear are so numerous in many areas they are considered predators. Canadian lynx, bobcats, wolves and foxes also are found. It is small wonder that Washington is one of the finest hunting states.

Among smaller animals is the strange "mountain beaver," which is not a beaver, but an animal that burrows in wet hillsides. It is found only in western Washington and Oregon. True beavers, once almost exterminated, now are making a comeback. A shrew-mole is an odd look alike combination of these two animals.

Among the more unusual birds are the horn-billed auklets. Destruction Island harbors about 10,000 of these relatives of the penguins, who like their southern relatives also always wear their "dress clothes." Innumerable shrilling gulls wheel and sail about, cleverly dropping clams on rocks from considerable height to open them. Other shore birds are sandpipers, avocets, turnstones and surfbirds. Sandhill cranes, American coots, and great blue heron are common. Ducks and geese are also plentiful. Inland birds are so numerous that a hundred species are found in the Mt. Rainier area alone. Among the most tuneful Washington

49

birds are the golden warbler, Audubon's warbler, and western lark. The willow goldfinch is the state bird.

From the fresh and salt waters of the state come almost innumerable varieties of fish. Five varieties of the invaluable salmon, of course, head the list. Much has been written about the mysteries of the salmon's life. They hatch in upper reaches of streams, go down those streams to the sea, and at the end of their lives come back to their birthplaces where they die after spawning. Salmon have been found in streams a thousand miles from the ocean. Sport anglers who catch salmon in Washington may experience the pleasure of having their catch canned right on the dock.

The steelhead trout is another prominent fish with migratory habits. Largest fresh water fish in North America are the mammoth sturgeon of the Columbia and Snake rivers. Silver trout, Colorado River smelt, halibut and tuna are all common in their respective waters. The hatcheries of Washington replenish the fish population with over fifty million fish per year.

Olympia oysters are famed around the world. These are the smallest on the market and the only oysters native to Washington. One man when served a plate of these oysters in a restaurant complained, "I ordered oysters, not baked beans!" Olympia oysters were almost exterminated a few years ago but have, fortunately, made a comeback. The coast is renowned for its clams—especially the giant geoduck and popular razor back.

Starfish of unusual size are frequently found, and even an occasional whale wanders into the dead end of Puget Sound and has to detour out again.

Growing Things

One-sixth of all the saw-timber in the United States is growing in Washington under conditions of perpetual yield. At least as much new growth comes each year as is taken away by lumbering. Among the most valuable of Washington trees are the majestic stands of Douglas fir and red cedar. The greatest stand of Douglas fir known in the Pacific Northwest was located in the region of Gray's Harbor. Douglas fir grows differently from other trees. Usually, trees of different ages grow together, but Douglas fir only grows thickly in even-aged stands because it will not thrive in the shade.

The useful lodgepole pine took its name from its use as a lodgepole in Indian tepees. It is especially strong in reseeding itself, and its cones can withstand even severe fire. Sitka spruce is another commercial tree.

Among the many deciduous trees of Washington, the western dogwood is one of the most popular, with its beautiful blossoms in spring and brilliant autumn color. Also admired are the white flowers and red berries of the madrona tree.

The Olympic peninsula has been called our largest remaining forested wilderness area. Here the temperate climate and enormous rainfall combine to create rain forests. In these both trees and underbrush grow luxuriantly; this kind of growth is related to that of jungles in tropical areas.

Plants of Washington range from desolate sagebrush, rabbit brush, antelope brush, and greasewood and prickly cactus to Alpine plants carpeting high meadows; from the sand dune plants of the coast to the lush bunchgrass of the Inland Empire; from the slukkish seaweed, rich in vitamins, eaten by the Indians, to swordfish fern, with its stems looming four feet above the ground.

Famed explorer and missionary Father Pierre De Smet admired Washington's state flower, the rhododendron, which he wrote grows like "bouquets of splendid flowers . . . thousands of them together." Rarer plants are the deerhead orchid and the very rare phantom orchid.

Captain William Clark was introduced to the salal when he received in a Clatsop Indian hut a bowl of "syrup pleasant to the taste made from a species of berry. . . . Of these berries a bread is also prepared . . ."

Scottish fur traders introduced the Scotch broom, and now it grows riotously in many of the western parts of the state.

The wide range of plants in Washington is illustrated by the fact that there are over seven hundred varieties of wildflowers in the Mt. Rainier region alone.

Minerals and Fossils

About thirty metallic minerals are found in Washington, including gold and silver, platinum, lead, zinc, copper, manganese, tungsten, molybdenum, and chromium, and sizeable quantities of iron ore.

Seventy nonmetallic minerals including building stone, clay, sand and gravel, cement, soapstone and talc, asbestos, marl, shell, and gem stones are also found there. One of the greatest mineral resources of the state is a six-billion-ton reserve of coal.

Among other outstanding mineral resources of the state must be listed its various rich soils, such as that of the Palouse country. "The most fertile irrigable land anywhere" is the description of the Grand Coulee region soils. These are said to be two to two-and-a-half times as productive as average soil.

Some authorities assert that the state's water and the waterpower available from it are far and away the greatest natural resource of Washington. The Columbia alone discharges twice as much as the total industrial water requirements of the nation, according to the State Department of Commerce. Total of underground reserves is greater than surface flow and surface reserves.

Unusual fossils of Washington include the Ginkgo Petrified Forest, discovered in 1932 by geologist George F. Beck. More varieties of petrified trees have been found in this region than in any other, with more than 75 prehistoric species so far identified. This forest is unusual in another way because the stone that has replaced the wood is opal rather than the more usual agate or calcite.

Fossilized remains of camels, pigs, cats, rodents and other prehistoric animals have been found, and dinosaur remains have been located in the San Juan Islands.

Collecting Your Thoughts

Which do you consider the most interesting animal, bird, fish or plant found in Washington?

From other sources list as many as you can of the kinds of fossils that have been found in Washington.

People Use Their Treasures

Water Means Food and Power

A sixth of all the water power potential in the United States is either developed or waiting for development in Washington. The state has far and away the largest water power capacity of all the states, 8,113,000 kilowatts developed as of 1962 and 18,600,000 estimated as yet undeveloped. Mighty power and irrigation dams dot the state, including Bonneville, Diablo, Chief Joseph, Wells, Rocky Reach, Wanapum, Priest Rapids, McNary, John Day, and The Dalles.

Greatest of Washington's dams, of course, is gigantic Grand Coulee, which includes the world's largest farmland reclamation effort, the Columbia Basin Project. A part of this project requires lifting millions of gallons of water over 280-foot-high cliffs into equalizing reservoirs in the Coulee area, using six of the greatest pumps ever developed. It is estimated that the areas (larger than Connecticut) reclaimed by the Columbia Basin Project may support a population of 1,200,000. The main dam, subsidiary dams, and the rest of the system, all combined, must be considered one of the wonders of the world. Its total cost is almost four hundred million dollars.

Wherever a new area of irrigation is brought in, new settlers come, and an expanding ring of green appears. When 600,000 acres of arid sagebrush lands became fertile with water, the Yakima valley leaped to prosperity almost overnight. When in 1903 the Highline Canal wound around the hills and tunneled through the mountains to refresh the Wenatchee Valley, much the same thing occurred.

One of the tricky problems in shutting off the river with great dams was that they would stop the migrating fish, particularly salmon. In order to provide passage for the fish, some dams have water staircases up which the fish progress. Others provided the fish with elevators. At Grand Coulee salmon are taken from the base of the dam and transported in water-conditioned tank trucks to spawn elsewhere.

A Host of Daffodils—Agriculture

Washington state has three distinct types of agriculture: dry land farming of eastern Washington, irrigated farming of central Washington, and the specialized farming of the heavy rainfall areas. More than $600,000,000 per year is earned by Washington farms. Of this, better than $125,000,000 comes from wheat. Washington wheat for the most part grows on fifteen inches of moisture a year. However, this moisture comes at exactly the right time of year—October through April. The Palouse region grows more wheat per acre than anywhere else. At harvest time vast seas of waving grain stretch as far as the eye can see. "Sailing" through yellow waves are combines, which now permit a few men to do the work of many in the wheat region.

Washington leads the world in apple production; it is first in the United States in hops, dry peas, green peas for processing, and rhubarb. About a fourth of all commercial apples produced in the United States are grown in Washington. Yakima, Chelan and Okanogan counties rank first, second and third in the country in apple production. These valleys

are picturesque in spring with clouds of pink blossoms. Roads in the regions appear to tunnel through endless orchards of foaming bloom. As the apples ripen many of the branches have to be propped up to keep them from breaking under the heavy load, even after thinning. In the fall the spicy odor of fruit is everywhere. Washington's annual apple crop is valued at $50,000,000.

Washing, grading, sorting, and packing provide jobs for swarms of seasonal workers who come in during the season. However, much of the work is now being done by machinery. Even apple-polishing is the work of a machine. The apples are stored in gigantic systems of cold rooms waiting for shipment. Apple wizards of Washington State University's Tree Fruit Experiment Station are constantly at work improving the apple crop and searching for new uses. Chemicals can now make a tree drop off its weaker blossoms in order not to over-produce in any one year. Other chemicals have been developed to hold the fruit on trees to fullest color, to produce bigger fruit, and to kill every kind of insect. Newly developed dwarf trees that produce years earlier are also easier to pick and thin. The experts have even developed a breakfast food made of apples, apple candy and other uses for the crop.

Other leading fruit crops include the strawberries of Kalama and Marysville and the cranberries of Greyland and Aberdeen. A fifth of all United States raspberries and blackberries are grown in Washington. One of the largest Concord vineyards in the country is Kennewick, known as the "grape juice capital of the Northwest."

Among the most spectacular crops of the state are those of the many bulb farms where vast fields of daffodils (50,000,000 per year), tulips and other bulb crops splash the countryside with color in spring. Whatcom County is called "Holland in America" because of its bulb farms cultivated by experienced people, many of Dutch background. Puyallup Valley is another leading bulb center.

In Whatcom and Skagit counties much of the United States cabbage, turnip, beet, and cauliflower seed is grown.

Livestock, poultry, and dairying are next to wheat in Washington's agricultural income. The Carnation Farms in King County boast the largest herd of registered Holsteins in the world. In such country cows can graze over the lush green meadows almost every day of the year.

Timber ! ! !

Washington ranks first in the production of wood pulp and third among the states in lumber and lumber products. According to the Washington Department of Commerce, "The prosperity of Washington, known as the Evergreen State, is based on its magnificent timberland resource. Over 67,000 persons are employed directly in the industry and thousands more are directly interested through transportation, the trades, construction and other industry."

About 240 billion board feet of Washington timber has been cut since the industry began, and about 315 billion remain.

Longview is known as one of the great timber centers of the world. The Weyerhauser Company conducts there the world's largest integrated forest products operation. Almost everything about the lumber industry is interesting to watch and to know about, including the huge appetites of the lumber crews, the picturesque operations in the forests with their "living crane" spar tree logging techniques, and such fascinating machines as the plywood lathes, which nimbly spin enormous logs while razor-sharp knives cut off a thin continuous flexible strip of wood.

Industrious and Ingenious

Washington is second among the eleven western states in industry. In the vital field of aluminum, Washington leads all states in production capacity because the vast electric power needed for aluminum smelting and rolling is available in the state.

A large user of aluminum, the Boeing Company, of Seattle, is the largest private employer in the state. From the small frail wire and fabric planes of 1916, the company has progressed to the rocket and space age with Bomarc, Dyna-soar and Minuteman.

Washington helped to usher in the atomic age in the Hanford atomic plant, with headquarters at the Atomic City—Richland. A new atomic power plant has been completed recently at Hanford to provide still another source of electricity for the Northwest. Although figures are not available, Washington probably ranks first in production of atomic materials.

The processing of food and food products, pulp and paper products, and lumbering machinery are other leading manufacturing industries of the state. The Puget Sound Naval Shipyard at Bremerton is the largest shipyard on the Pacific Coast. Other big shipyards are at Seattle, Everett, and Tacoma.

Fishing is still big business in Washington. Fish and shellfish worth more than forty million dollars come from its waters each year. Washington ranks fourth as a producer of canned fish and by-products. However, if its participation in the Alaska fishing industry were taken into consideration, Washington would rank first. More than seventy-five per cent of all persons engaged in the Alaskan fishing industry have their homes in Washington, and most fish companies of Alaska have their headquarters in Seattle.

Of course, the most valuable fish taken in Washington waters is salmon. A recent salmon harvest after processing was estimated to be worth almost $25,000,000. The shellfish harvest amounts to $10,000,000 annually. Kelso is one of the principal smelt centers of the world. A whaling fleet still operates from Bellevue on Lake Washington.

Since mining began in Washington, more than a billion and a half dollars worth of minerals have been taken from the soil and processed.

Annual value of mineral products in the state is more than $60,000,000. Washington leads the nation in production of magnesite. Some gold is still being produced. The largest combined copper smelter and refinery in the United States is at Tacoma. Clay and clay products, coal, limestone, sand and gravel add substantial amounts to the state's income. Even Epsom salts are mined near Oroville.

Transportation and Communication

One of the most picturesque periods of transportation occurred in the early time of the steamboat in the Northwest. In 1836 the *Beaver* of Hudson's Bay Company was the first steamer in the Pacific. Before long, steamers were operating on the Columbia and many of its tributaries. There were even steamers on the far-off Okanogan River. Where falls and rapids could not be passed, goods and passengers were portaged around to where another steamer took over. The first railroad in Washington, operating in 1851, was a wooden-railed affair making the portage around Celilo Falls of the Columbia.

First regular steamship service from San Francisco to Washington began in 1867, from Washington to Alaska in 1886, and to the Orient in 1891. One of the world's largest ferryboat fleets is operated by the state throughout Puget Sound. There are twenty-five port districts in the state, including Tacoma, Longview, Vancouver, and Seattle.

Seattle is known as "one of the world's greatest maritime cities." In addition to Elliott Bay, Seattle provides the fresh water shipping complex of Lakes Union, Washington, Portage and Salmon Bays, connected by the Lake Washington Ship Canal and Chittenden Locks, finished in 1916. There are 193 miles of waterfront in Seattle. Tacoma's Harbor of Commencement Bay is one of the best natural harbors in the country.

As a whole, the Puget Sound area might be considered one of the greatest transportation centers anywhere, with its terminals of transcontinental railroads, steamships and airlines operating overseas on the Great Circle air route to the Orient. Seattle-Tacoma International Airport was opened in 1949 at an original cost of $15,000,000. Much more has since been spent to keep it one of the leading jet terminals anywhere. The leap from prairie schooner to Boeing 707 took less than a hundred years. The first mail service was dispatched across Puget Sound in a canoe paddled by nine Indians. Today it takes little more time to send a letter halfway around the world. Actually, the first round-the-world flight began and ended at the Seattle Naval Base.

The role of railroads has already been partially discussed. The first steam railroad reached Washington in 1863. One of the earliest railroads was the Walla Walla and Columbia Railroad. It used a collie dog as one of its crew. His job was to run ahead of the train and frighten cattle from the right of way.

Coming of automobiles brought a need for better roads, and now the highway system of Washington is unmatched. One of the main difficulties in highway construction was crossing the Cascades. Today three main routes pierce the mountain reaches, with Snoqualmie Pass the heaviest traveled artery between east and west Washington.

Washington continued its transportation progress in 1962 when one of the world's first modern commercial monorail systems began operating at Seattle in 1962 to connect the world's fair with downtown.

First really fast communication between Washington and the rest of the country came with the opening of the first transcontinental telegraph in 1864. It was preceded by the first newspaper in 1852—the *Columbian* of Olympia.

Tourism is rapidly becoming an important source of income in the state. Almost seven million tourists a year spend an estimated $300,000,000 during their stay in Washington.

Collecting Your Thoughts

In addition to steam generators fired by coal, two other major types of electric power are used in Washington. Name these and list advantages of all three types.

If you were planning to buy a farm in Washington, what crop or crops would you want to raise?

Research is constantly discovering new uses for wood; read more on this subject.

Why is Washington a great transportation center?

Human Treasures

"Men of Old Were Brave and Bold"

Of all the neglected leaders of American history, Dr. John McLoughlin is one of the most notable. His biographer, Richard G. Montgomery, has said, "Of all the heroic figures of the early West, Dr. John McLoughlin was the most remarkable. As a leader, a benefactor, and a Christian, he was unrivaled; and, though his life ended in tragedy, the passage of time has not only enhanced his greatness but placed him within the charmed circle of our national heroes."

In the midst of a wilderness he created a remarkable circle of civilization, and became almost a god to the Indians—who honored him for his firmness and fairness. Through his business genius he brought a great fortune to the company he served for most of his life. He became renowned throughout the west for his great compassion and great generosity—"a man of limitless patience, cool and just and kind."

Forced from his position, he became an American and made his home in Oregon where he died after being deprived of most of his property. It remained for future generations to rediscover "The great spirit that could not see suffering and that sought to conciliate and ward off war."

Even more tragic was the life of Dr. Marcus Whitman, whose life ended in one of the most violent episodes of our history, his life work apparently of little account. Yet his statue stands in the national Capitol at Washington, D.C., selected by the people of the state of Washington to represent them in the nation's Hall of Fame.

This tribute, of course, is due partly to the gallant bravery with which both Marcus and Narcissa Whitman steadfastly faced the dangers and disappointments of a hostile country for ten years. More importantly, however, as a representative of his country in one of the farthest outposts of America, as a man devoted to spreading the best of American life as well as religion, Marcus Whitman performed a noble service for humanity, one that has been equalled by few.

Another remarkable missionary, of a later period, was Father Etienne de Rouge, who devoted most of his personal fortune to the founding of St. Mary's Mission in 1889 near Okanogan. He was greatly beloved by the Indians he served, and is said to have celebrated the Mass in a mixture of Chinook jargon and Latin to help the Indians understand it. He insisted that his parishioners wear their hats in church, and it made a strange sight to see the congregation with long braids descending below their tilted headgear, intently listening to one of the earliest services in the vernacular.

One of the earliest scientists in the region was David Douglas, a young Scot who studied Nature for the Royal Horticultural Society of London. In 1825 he wrote, "Having resolved to devote a season in the interior parts of the country skirting with Rocky Mountains, Dr. John McLoughlin, who was unremitting with his kind attentions, allowed me to embark in the spring boat for the interior with two reams of paper, which was an enormous indulgence."

Dr. Douglas was apt to wander absent mindedly in the woods. To protect him, Dr. McLoughlin indicated to the Indians that this was the famous "grass man" with great powers over natural forces. In all his wanderings he was never harmed because of Dr. McLoughlin's little story. Among Douglas' many contributions was naming the Cascade Mountains, and, of course, his name now graces the magnificent Douglas fir.

Other scientists and explorers included the famed John C. Frémont, who came down the Columbia in 1843 on a raft, and Colonel Benjamin Louis Eulalie Bonneville, who was given great prominence in the writings of Washington Irving. Bonneville arrived at Fort Vancouver in 1834. Irving credits him with being the first man to lead a wagon party over the Cascades. His name, of course, is given to the great dam across the Columbia.

The Dispossessed

Some of the most interesting Indian leaders are those who take their places in the history of Washington.

Probably the best known of these is Hallshallakeen, Eagle Wing, better known as Chief Joseph the younger. The older Joseph was a mighty chief of the Nez Perce in the last days of their great influence and power. Hallshallakeen was born in what is now Washington where Joseph Creek meets the Grande Ronde River in the region where

Washington, Idaho and Oregon join.

He and his father had remained loyal to the United States in spite of many injustices by settlers and the government. At last the younger Joseph and his people revolted, for the first time in their history, and they started off on the tragic journey to Canada. In Washington today, the names of the Josephs are found in many places throughout the state.

Another tragic Indian figure was good Chief Garry of the Spokane Indians. At the Red River Mission school, Chief Garry had become a zealous convert to Presbyterianism. He returned to his people in 1830 and set up a school to teach them the new religion as well as English and agriculture. By 1887 the flood of settlers had dispossessed Chief Garry and his people. In later years the aged chief rode his white horse about the streets of Spokane asking for food to keep himself and his blind wife alive. Not until many years after his death was this physically small, proud and kindly man honored with a granite memorial in Greenwood Cemetery.

Chief Seattle was a particularly able leader who served as the elected chief of six tribes, a post he held because of his remarkable ability. Over six feet tall, he made an impressive appearance and was an able orator and man of great vision. He, too, is remembered with a granite memorial over his grave at Suquamish, on which is inscribed "firm friend of the Whites and for him the City of Seattle was named by its Founders."

Chief Tslalakum of Whidbey Island made a long trip to ask Father Francois Blanchet to bring religion to his people. Although he could not go to Whidbey just then, Father Blanchet made a book of Bible stories in pictures, telling Chief Tslalakum what each picture meant. When

Father Blanchet visited Whidbey Island the next year, he was amazed to find the Indians singing hymns and carrying out the Catholic rituals he had taught their chief. They presented him with a huge wooden cross. Tslalakum told him that they had beaten another tribe in battle and considered they had the victory because they knew God.

Other prominent Washington Indian names include Kamiakin, Yakima chief who began crude irrigation in the valley, Chief Patkanim of the Salish Indians who fought for the whites and has a totem pole erected to his memory, Chief Moses for whom Moses Coulee is named, and Chief Red Wolf who planted the first orchard in the Snake River Valley. Still remembered is the wealthy Indian John Hoate who died penniless through giving too many potlaches.

Creative Spirits

Writers associated with Washington have won many honors. Winners of the Pulitzer Prize have included Vernon Louis Parrington, who won the prize in 1928 for his *Main Currents in American Thought*. Audrey Wurdemann's *Bright Ambush* was awarded the Pulitzer Prize for poetry in 1935. Another Pulitzer poetry winner was Theodore Roethke, in 1954, for *The Waking*.

One of the most popular writers of humor was Betty MacDonald, whose *The Egg and I* and other lighthearted books won for her an enormous following. An earlier author was Frederick Homer Balch, who caused considerable stir with his book *The Bridge of the Gods*. He is buried at Lyle. Ella Higginson gained a national reputation with her fiction and verse. Biographical works of Edward Wagenknecht are well known.

Led by Mark Tobey, Seattle has become the center for the "widely acclaimed Northwest School of Painting." Another prominent Washington painter was Gustave Sohon, who in the 1850's created the only existing portraits of many early Indian leaders.

Such Interesting People

William Boeing was a young businessman who got into the aircraft business through repairing his damaged plane in a rented shed. From this beginning he built one of the great manufacturing enterprises of our time. Another Washington aviation pioneer is Moulton B. Taylor, developer of the Aerocar, a combination automobile and plane.

Another Seattle inventor, William Dubilier, duplicated independently a number of discoveries in radio of radio pioneer Lee De Forest. Dubilier set up a broadcasting transmitter at Seattle as early as 1912. Inventor of a different type was John Bennett, of Bellingham, early horticulturist who developed the Bennett pear and many other fruits and flowers. George Pocock of Seattle is a famed designer of racing shells.

The dream of lumber magnate Robert Alexander Long resulted in the creation of a model community—named in his honor—Longview. Another "builder" was Ezra Meeker, who laid out many towns. As an old man, in 1911, in a covered wagon Meeker retraced his route of pioneer days over the Oregon Trail.

Another pioneer town builder was George Washington, a Negro brought to Washington Territory as a slave. Freed by his owner, who later adopted him, George Washington built a house and developed the town of Centralia. He sold lots at $10 each, with one lot free to any buyer who would build a house. George Washington Park at Centralia was donated by the town's founder, and now commemorates him.

Olympic pioneer F. N. Streeter struggled into the high Olympics carrying only a mattock and sack of potatoes. He planted the potatoes and waited for his wife who walked along the coast and up into the mountains carrying their baby.

Washington claims radio and television star, Mary Livingston, and opera diva Patrice Munsel. A pioneer Washington family has produced a number of show people, including one of the best-known names of the modern world—Harry Lillis Crosby, better known as "Bing."

Collecting Your Thoughts

Many young Washington leaders are becoming prominent in many fields and some will certainly rank with the greatest leaders of the past. Read about as many of these as you can and make your own list of future leaders. You might want to keep this for reference later.

Teaching and Learning

Cushing Eells had been forced to leave his Tshimakain Mission after the Whitman Massacre. In later years he determined that a college should be founded at Waiilatpu in tribute to Dr. and Mrs. Whitman. This dream became almost his whole existence. In 1859 the legislature gave a charter for Whitman Seminary, and with the almost superhuman help of Eells this became the first college in what is now Washington. Eells wrote in his journal, "Day and night I cry for favor for Whitman College . . . Dreamed of the College . . . It seemed that the agony was so great that body and spirit would part." The Whitman College thrives at Walla Walla today—a tribute to two devoted men. Its Conservatory of Music, oldest in the Northwest, is particularly renowned.

The University of Washington opened at Seattle in 1861 with Asa S. Mercer as both teacher and president. It had financial difficulty for

many years. The smallness of the faculty was responsible for one of the best-known anecdotes on education. Renowned Harvard educator Charles W. Eliot was visiting the University of Washington and asked a professor what chair he held in the university. "I teach astronomy, botany, physics, zoology. . . ." Dr. Eliot interrupted him, "You don't hold a chair; you occupy a settee!"

At another time someone commented about the white fence built around the campus and was told this was to "keep the stumps from getting out." Some early students were allowed to pay their tuition with cords of wood.

Today's mammoth institution of about 20,000 students is a far cry from those early beginnings. Its dynamic spirit is shown by some of the unique specialized work done there. Its College of Fisheries is one of the few to offer degrees in this subject. Here some of the most important studies of salmon are being undertaken. The university's center at Hanford is devoted to study of nuclear technology. The university also operates a gigantic and much respected Health Science Center.

One of the nation's outstanding drama schools is that of the university. Its unusual theater was built like a showboat. The Drama College is said to have originated the idea of "theater-in-the-round" so popular today. The university's rowing crews, training on Lake Washington, are a favorite sight.

When the state was ready to open an agricultural and mechanical arts college, a group of commissioners visited several possible locations. When they visited the town of Pullman, the people had determined that they would all be out on the streets to impress the commission with what a bustling and lively community they operated. They also offered 150 acres of land and $12,000 in cash. The commissioners must have been impressed because Washington State College opened at Pullman in 1892. This is now the Washington State University. The State Farm has helped in many notable agricultural developments, especially the creation of new varieties of wheat for the region. Western Washington Experiment Station of the university at Puyallup is an outstanding division of the university. The university also operates a notable nuclear research reactor.

There are thirteen private colleges and universities in Washington including Gonzaga University and Fort Wright College, formerly Holy Names College, Spokane; Seattle University, one of the west's largest Catholic universities; Saint Martin's College, Olympia; University of Puget Sound and Pacific Lutheran University, Tacoma; Seattle Pacific College; Whitworth College, Spokane; and Walla Walla College. The three other state operated institutions are Western Washington State College, Bellingham; Central Washington State College, Ellensburg; and Eastern Washington State College, Chene.

There are fifteen public junior colleges and one private junior college—Tacoma Catholic Junior College—in Washington. Broadway Edison Technological School, Seattle, has been called "one of the best of its kind." Anne Wright Seminary is said to be one of the outstanding girls' schools in the Pacific Northwest.

First formal education in what is now Washington was established by Dr. John McLoughlin at Vancouver in 1832. Chief Garry's school at Spokane was next in 1833. Narcissa Whitman opened her school at Waiilatpu in 1837. The first territorial legislature in 1854 passed a law providing for free public schools. In early days schools were a community project. Building of the school at Spangle was typical. Everyone set to work, and within a day the walls and roof were finished. Handmade desks and benches were provided. When the building was finished, there was a day-long celebration of racing, story-telling and feasting, topped by an orchestra of a reed organ, three violins and a harmonica.

Modern public schools in Washington are among the best administered and most competently staffed in the country. The Washington school system is particularly renowned for its work in curriculum building and reconstruction. Some educators consider the Washington curriculum work as the world's most outstanding in this field.

Collecting Your Thoughts

Find as many reasons as you can as to why the schools of Washington are rated so highly by educators.

Enchantment of Washington

A Mighty Voice—Seattle

The poet Wordsworth wrote, "Two voices are there; one is of the sea, one of the mountains; each a mighty voice." Few cities hear both of these voices so strongly as Seattle, nestled among the sparkling reaches of Puget Sound, with majestic mountains towering to the east and looming across the Sound to the west. Such a setting gives Seattle justification for its claim as one of the world's most beautiful cities.

The importance of Seattle as the metropolis of the northwest seems even more striking when it is remembered that the entire growth of the city has come in little more than one long lifetime. Rolland H. Denny, son of one of the founding families, came in his mother's arms as a two-month-old infant when there was no community at all on Elliott Bay. He lived to see this become a city of almost half a million before his death—the largest city of its age in the world.

Seattle's first industry was Henry Yesler's sawmill at Pioneer Square; a coffee barrel served as its first bank. In the early days there were many hardships and shortages of almost everything, including unmarried women. Seattle first gained wide fame when civic leader Asa Mercer went east to try and remedy this shortage. Although many suspected him, he was able to persuade eleven young ladies from good families to come back to Seattle to find husbands.

The bachelors of Seattle turned out, as one account says, "looking like grizzlies in store clothes and their hair slicked down like sea otters." Two years later forty-six additional ladies were brought to Seattle. Among these, Mercer himself found a wife. Many of Seattle's leading families proudly trace their background to the "Mercer Girls."

As the city grew, the business district was restricted by hills. During a thirty year period, the city sluiced away more than forty million cubic yards of hills and used the dirt to fill in tidal flats for factory sites. The unique ship canal and locks brought the inland fresh water lakes into use as sea ports, and one of the most ambitious programs of any city saw the creation of the city's power project on the Skagit River.

Other outstanding engineering works include two of the world's five floating bridges. In 1963 the longest and heaviest floating structure in the world was opened—the Evergreen Bridge across Lake Washington. It joined the previous record holder, the older Lake Washington Floating Bridge. Another floating bridge crosses the Hood Canal, not far from Seattle.

Visitors to the city today marvel at Seattle's moderate temperature. In a city as far north as St. John's, Newfoundland, azaleas, camellias and rhododendrons flourish. Only twice has Seattle's temperature passed the hundred mark, and it has never reached zero.

Among the most interesting tourist centers is the area where the world's fair was held in 1962. No other world's fair was ever planned to leave such a permanent legacy. The 74-acre, park-like fairground is now called the Seattle Center. Dominating the city is the Space Needle. This 600-foot tower features an outside elevator and a restaurant on top which revolves, giving the diners a complete turn around the city's magnificent vistas every hour. The "Eye of the Needle" restaurant is so neatly balanced that a one-horse-power motor turns it easily. Seattle people watch the flaming gas torch on top of the Needle for news of the weather. The flame's colors are changed chemically to show weather changes.

The fair's United States Science Exhibit has now become a permanent scientific museum—The Pacific Science Center, showing the "Five Worlds of Science." The Food Circus at the center offers dozens of varieties of domestic and foreign dishes. In the Performing Arts group are three buildings, a 3,000 seat Opera House, a playhouse and arena. Sports and recreation events are held in a 12,000 seat stadium, where most admissions are free.

Outstanding Northwest artists and craftsmen exhibit their creations in the Arts and Crafts Center. One of the world's most spectacular fountains is the International Fountain at the center of the grounds. Its 230 jets of water arch 100 feet high in constantly changing patterns, accompanied by carillon music. At night changing colored lights play on the surging waters.

Reaching Seattle Center can be a novel thrill if the monorail is used. This is the United States' first operating municipal monorail service. By monorail, the Seattle Center is only a few minutes from downtown Seattle and its shops. In Pike Place Market is a picturesque collection of

PACIFIC SCIENCE CENTER

bazaars where everything from squid and octopus to imported dried flowers may be purchased in the colorful stalls.

Ye Olde Curiosity Shoppe is a landmark of the Northwest. Here the most unusual merchandise can be found. One of the shop's displays (not for sale) is the mummy of a prospector who died in the desert, where the body was preserved still showing the bullet wound which brought about his death.

Less gruesome are the collections of the many fine Seattle museums, including the Museum of History and Industry, and Seattle Art Museum. The art museum was given to the city by Dr. Richard E. Fuller and his mother. It has one of the world's finest collections of oriental art, particularly Chinese jade.

Seattle's cultural life is also enriched by music and the theater. As early as 1895 a performance of *Pinafore* was given using a scow on Lake Washington for a stage, with the audience seated on the beach. Now there is a permanent Aqua Theater on Green Lake. The drama department of the University of Washington is noted for some of the most important advances of dramatic art, theater design, and staging.

Organized in 1903, the Seattle Symphony became an orchestra of international recognition in 1940 when renowned conductor Sir Thomas Beecham became its conductor.

Seattle has outstanding parks of great variety. Schmitz Park is an unspoiled wilderness area in a metropolitan center. The University of Washington Arboretum in Washington Park contains 250 acres of extraordinary plantings and a lovely Japanese tea garden. Its Rhododendron Glen is a nine acre wonderland of gorgeous bloom in season. The zoo in Woodland Park includes almost 1900 animals.

The campus of the University of Washington is one of the country's most beautiful. Its library museum is especially renowned for an Alaska collection containing many rare Russian manuscripts. One of the best-known statues of George Washington is that by Lorado Taft, at the university.

Seattle is noted for its water festivals. For Opening Day on Lake Washington, a sort of maritime Mardi Gras, a procession of brightly decorated boats and costumed crews sails through the canal and into the lake. Then the year's first sailboat race is run. Later, the unlimited

hydroplane race on Lake Washington in August is one of the great events of its kind. In December the parade of the brightly decorated Christmas ship followed by other boats, one bringing Santa Claus, is always eagerly awaited by the youngsters.

Residents of Seattle are as much at home on water as on land. In fact many of them live in houseboats, some of great cost and elegance. Seattle has more pleasure boats per capita than any other community. New residents are often advised to "turn your car in on a boat." Innumerable ferry rides and cruises on the Sound, to the San Juan and to Canada, add to the maritime flavor of the city.

Chief Seattle's namesake city honors the Indian leader with a bronze statue by James A. Wehn, in the center of Denny Place. The outstretched hand of the statue indicates that he was a "tillicum" (friend). A modern Seattle organization called the Tillicums aims to retain for their city its reputation as one of the "friendliest" anywhere.

Other Sights of the Sound

Puget Sound is one of the most beautiful inland seas in the world, and one of the world's great recreational areas.

In 1833 the Hudson's Bay Company built old Fort Nisqually about eighteen miles south of present Tacoma. In recent years the old fort was moved to a new site, rebuilt and restored. In 1841 Charles Wilkes (discoverer of Antarctica) began a survey of Puget Sound in the region and named the bay where he started "Commencement Bay," considered one of the world's outstanding deep-water harbors. Tacoma grew up on this harbor. Nicholas De Lin built the first sawmill there, and the neighboring Indians crowded about with so much curiosity they had to be pushed away so the men could work.

73

Modern Tacoma is home of the outstanding Historical Museum of the State Historical Society, largest of its kind in the West. The Ferry Museum of Art in Tacoma was established while Washington was still a territory. Another cultural highlight is the Tacoma Symphony.

Among Tacoma attractions is the tallest totem pole in the world—105 feet—carved by Alaska Indian experts. Point Defiance Park is the largest virgin forest area in a metropolitan setting. This 640 acres of unspoiled wilderness has 200-feet-high Douglas firs and other magnificent specimens. In some areas of the park, nothing has been planted by man. The Point Defiance Aquarium has a large collection of marine specimens.

The nation's first municipally owned moving sidewalk is known as the Tacoma Escalades. Another engineering wonder is the Tacoma Narrows Bridge, replacing the former bridge known as Galloping Gertie, because of its swinging and swaying in heavy winds. One of these winds caused Gertie to collapse in 1940 in one of the most spectacular disasters of its kind.

TACOMA NARROWS BRIDGE

Outstanding annual festival at Tacoma is the Daffodil Festival, with its mammoth parade.

Steilacoom, chartered in 1853, is the oldest incorporated community in the state. Here was founded the first Protestant church north of the Columbia. Fort Lewis, named in honor of pioneer explorer Meriwether Lewis, is the second largest permanent army post in the country.

Hood Canal bends its fishhook shape along a narrow eighty-mile long course. At night the waters often shimmer with the eerie glow of phosphorescence.

Heartbeat of Bremerton is the Puget Sound Navy Yard, which can be viewed in a conducted tour, highlighted by a visit to the *U.S.S. Missouri,* now permanently anchored there. Visitors may view the site on deck where General Douglas MacArthur received the surrender of the Japanese ending World War II. Ship models, pictures and other displays of naval history are exhibited in the shipyard's museum.

Mountains of the Gods—Olympic Peninsula

Ever since explorer John Meares decided the mountains between Puget Sound and the Pacific were fit for the gods, other awed visitors have been agreeing with him. One of the most inspiring views anywhere is that of the Olympics from knife-like Hurricane Ridge, where a jumble of mountains can be seen pushing through the clouds as far as the eye can follow. A lodge there permits visitors to spend time comfortably in this region.

The Olympic Peninsula contains several Indian reservations, national forests, a number of good-sized towns and the Olympic National Park. Here are fifty-six species of mammals, including such strange contrasts as majestic elk and ocean-going seals. The west side of the Olympic Mountains is the wettest area in the continental United States, while the east slope is the driest part of the Pacific Coast.

Although not of great height, the Olympics rise so steeply that abrupt drops of 3,000 feet are not unusual, and a number of these mountains have yet to be climbed for the first time.

Port Angeles is the leading city of the Olympic Peninsula. This region was set aside by President Lincoln as a second District of Columbia, but the order was later revoked. Now the city is known as the Gateway to Olympic National Park, which spreads across the horizon, like a majestic stage setting rising almost from the edge of deep blue waters.

Potlach on the Hood Canal is headquarters for the Skokomish Indian Reservation. Many of the Indian community belong to the Shaker faith which is said to have been founded by an Indian, John Slocum. The chant and ceremonial dances of their religious ritual are not open to the public.

The Capital

Olympia, capital of Washington, was founded by a fisherman, Edmund Sylvester, and a Presbyterian divinity student, Levi Lathrop. After the Indian wars the settlers of Olympia removed a wooden stockade they had made for protection and planked the streets with its timbers.

Today the capital city is a park-like community dominated by the 287 foot dome of the Legislative Building (Capitol). This dome is the fourth highest dome in the world and one of two in the United States made of solid stone. Inside the dome hangs a massive Tiffany chandelier weighing five tons. The acoustics in the dome are so good that regular organ recitals are given there. The lavishly ornamented building was completed in 1928 at a cost of almost seven and a half million dollars.

Included in the Capitol group are the monumental Temple of Justice, a general administrative building, State Library, Museum, and other buildings. The expanding Capitol grounds, known as the campus, has

flower gardens with Japanese cherry trees, a totem pole, and a rare Ginkgo Biloba tree. An exact duplicate of the famous Danish Tivoli Gardens fountain was added to the Capitol grounds in 1953, gift of the Olympia-Tumwater Foundation. The World War I Memorial Monument was dedicated in 1938. On the museum grounds is the Lone Tree-Conover monument, dedicated to Charles T. Conover, a historian who was first to call Washington the "Evergreen State."

On an island in Capital Lake visitors flock to see one of the nation's largest Christmas displays—called Christmas Isle—created each year by Olympia groups and Fort Lewis personnel.

Northwest Washington

The northwest corner of Washington State has been removed as if chewed out by the sea. In that sea stand the tops of 172 mountains now known as the San Juan Islands. From the air, someone has said that the San Juans look like a "parade of prehistoric sea monsters." The region is classed with the world's most beautiful marine scenery. During the fourteen year "Pig War," the pig was the only casualty. The San Juans are the last place the British flag flew in what is now the United States.

The islands range in size from the largest, Orcas, to tiny sea-dashed rocks such as dome-shaped Towhead Island, home of two eagles for many years. Mount Constitution on Orcas Island rises 2,409 feet above sea level, and a magnificent view of the islands may be had from the observation tower on its summit. Friday Harbor, on San Juan Island, is the largest town in the islands.

Neighboring Whidbey Island was named for Joseph Whidbey, who discovered the pass which makes it an island. Narrow Deception Pass was given that name when Whidbey discovered that it was not a closed harbor. The pass is noted for its swift and racing tides. Two hundred Indians who had never seen a white man could not believe that Whidbey had white skin. They thought he must be covered with white ashes. He had to open his shirt to convince them that he was white all over. Whidbey Island Naval Air Station is the largest naval air base in the Northwest.

Metropolis of northwest Washington is Bellingham, named for Sir William Bellingham by George Vancouver. Beautiful Chuckanut Drive along Chuckanut Bay has been called a "wonder road" because of the difficulty of cutting it into the mountainsides and because of its beautiful vistas of scenery. At Bellingham is the house where Captain George Pickett lived for a time.

Near Bellingham is the Lummi Indian Reservation. The Lummi-Stommish Water Carnival is one of the popular festivals of the Northwest. Feature of this event is the exciting race of war canoes, through Hale Passage in Puget Sound. These are manned by eleven-man crews of Indians descended from the original inhabitants of the area. Some of the hollowed cedar log war canoes are fifty feet long. Hundreds of Indians attend the festival which features also many other sports. Some come from great distances.

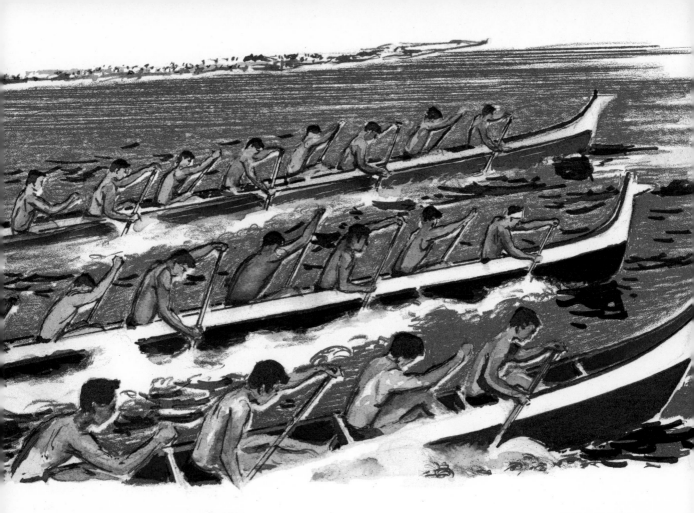

At the Swinomish Indian Reservation near Mt. Vernon a three day tribal festival is held. The native dances are spectacular, featuring frenzied solo dancers—with feathers flying and bone bracelets jangling— wailing chants, throbbing tom-toms and dramatic pauses.

On the Canadian-United States border near Blaine, the International Peace Arch was erected as a symbol of the long period of calm relations between the two neighboring countries. The Danielson Library at Blaine is unique for its thousand volumes in the Icelandic language.

Mt. Baker was named for Joseph Baker, a lieutenant of George Vancouver. Its slopes are popular both winter and summer. Even in July a ski tournament is held there. Glacier Peak looms in a remote region far from any highways.

North—Northeast

Beautiful Lake Chelan is dagger shaped, glacier carved, enormously deep and the largest natural lake in Washington. Actually, however, the lake is formed by a natural dam. When the glaciers melted they left an earth and rock mound, called a moraine, which dammed the Chelan River. Today a man-made dam across the four-mile-long river raises the lake still higher for power purposes.

A boat or ferry trip up the length of Lake Chelan, between the Chelan and Sawtooth ranges, is one of the country's great travel experiences.

Gigantic Grand Coulee Dam, center of Grand Coulee Recreation Area, is the number two tourist attraction of the state, ranking next to Mt. Rainier. This gigantic structure strides across the Columbia to a length of 4,000 feet. Over its spillway crashes a cascade of water twice as high as Niagara Falls. At night huge banks of floodlights, fed by power generated by the dam itself, transform the dam into a colored fairyland. Franklin D. Roosevelt Lake created by the dam backs up the waters of the Columbia for 151 miles almost to the Canadian border. Grand Coulee and Electric City are the communities nearest the dam itself.

Dry Falls State Park attracts visitors to the region where the ancient Columbia River once rumbled to form the greatest waterfall in history.

GRAND COULEE DAM

SPOKANE

Seat of an Empire

Spokane is the trading center for a vast region known as the "Inland Empire," stretching from the Cascades to the Rockies, from far to the south to across the border into Canada. This great region is almost twice the size of the state of Washington.

Spokane occupies the natural site for the leadership of this empire. In past years the trails of the Indians met at the falls of the Spokane River, and this is also the only place in four hundred miles at which the mountains can be crossed on an easy grade. Consequently, five transcontinental rail lines and many highways now replace the ancient Indian trails where the metropolis of the Inland Empire meets the river. This city of almost 200,000 population claims to be the nation's friendliest community. This may be partly due to the climate, which is compared to New Mexico's in the winter and Maine's in summer.

When water is high enough in the river, Spokane Falls is one of the city's major sights, with the river roaring over the boulders in a series of cascades. At night these are brilliantly lighted. Many people, even some living in the region, do not know that there is another river—underground—flowing in almost the same course as the above-ground river. Power generated on the upper one is used to pump Spokane's crystal-pure spring water from the underground river.

83

Recreational facilities in the Spokane area are almost unsurpassed. A group of civic leaders purchased Mt. Spokane and presented it to the city for a park, so that Spokane now is one of an elite group of cities owning their own mountains. There is an inspiring view from the top of Mt. Spokane, and in winter it is a skiing paradise, with a mile-long chair lift.

The area of parks in Spokane is larger per person than in any other city of the United States. In Coeur d'Alene Park grows at least one tree of every native variety in the Northwest. Cliff Park was formed around an ancient volcanic island. Seventy-six crystal lakes sparkle within a fifty mile radius of the city.

Cultural events have long had strong support in Spokane. In 1883 famed opera star Emma Abbott gave a performance of the *Bohemian Girl* at Spokane. There was no theater, so a warehouse was used, with nail kegs for seats. A sold-out house gladly paid $2.00 each to sit on nail kegs. For years Spokane's five-story auditorium was the finest theater west of the Mississippi. Today residents of Spokane are proud of their Spokane Philharmonic Orchestra.

One of the outstanding church structures of the Northwest is Episcopal Cathedral of St. John the Evangelist in Spokane.

The city's annual Lilac Festival features two parades—one at night by torchlight—a flower show, and other highlights. The Spokane Interstate Fair attracts visitors from many states and Canada.

Southeast

Pullman was named for George Pullman of railroad sleeping-car fame. The Pullman region has become one of the outstanding university centers, particularly in view of the small population of its area. This is due to the close proximity of the Washington State University at Pullman and the University of Idaho at Moscow, just over the state line.

From Dayton one of the few roads may be taken into the almost completely unspoiled Blue Mountains. This is the Skyline Highway, running along the "backbone" of the mountains.

Major goal of many travelers in the southeast section of Washington is a visit to the graves of martyred Marcus and Narcissa Whitman where their mission of Waiilatpu once stood near present Walla Walla. The mass grave site of the Waiilatpu massacre victims is now a national monument, and a museum of relics of the mission is located there.

Walla Walla was until 1880 the largest city in Washington Territory. In 1859 it became the county seat of Walla Walla County, including half of what is now the state. At Walla Walla is a statue of Chief Lawyer, who saved the life of Territorial Governor Stevens at the parley with the Indians held where the city is now. Indian language Walla Walla means many waters; however, its boosters claim they liked the place so much they named it twice.

Richland, Pasco, and Kennewick are known as the Tri-Cities. They occupy a unique location from the standpoint of geography, which might be known as the Tri-Rivers. Within a few miles, three of the continent's great rivers come together—the Columbia, Snake, and Yakima. The new Federal Building at Richland features one of the few displays anywhere showing with considerable detail how nuclear energy is created. The mushroom growth of Richland—homes, schools, shops, and all the facilities needed by a large city—was almost unique in history. The federal ownership and operation of the community was also a novel feature. Today Richland has become a thriving "permanent" city where lawns and growing shade trees now flourish, irrigated by Columbia River waters.

Kennewick Highland project has made Kennewick the center for an irrigated area of 20,000 acres. The project has transformed sage country into a rich growing region. The city is center of the state's grape industry. Its name, meaning "Winter Paradise," is usually thought to be appropriate.

Pasco is a rail center and the best headquarters for visits to Ice Harbor Lock and Dam of the Snake River and the great McNary Dam straddling the Columbia. Near Pasco is Sacajawea State Park, paying tribute to the devoted Indian woman who guided the Lewis and Clark party across the Rocky Mountains.

In midsummer the Tri-Cities unite for one of the largest festivals of the region—the Tri-City Water Follies, a talent show, swimming competition, boat racing, and water carnival.

Central and Southwest

Wenatchee and Yakima were built on apples, but now other crops and other industries have helped to give the region additional sources of income, such as the aluminum smelter and casting plant at Wenatchee.

Yakima calls itself the "fruit bowl of the nation." The city took much pride in the fact that the country's first aluminum hotel was opened there in 1949. The city's name comes from the Yakima Indians, who now live on a reservation near Toppenish.

Ellensburg is the site of one of the country's best-known annual rodeos. A unique soldiers memorial has been erected near Goldendale. This takes the form of the prehistoric British ruins of Stonehenge, and is known as the Stonehenge Memorial. Near Maryhill is Maryhill Castle, planned by wealthy Samuel Hill. He built the great residence on a desolate spot overlooking the gorge of the Columbia River. Suddenly he decided to convert it into a museum, and Queen Marie of Rumania took part in the dedication.

North of the Columbia the rugged region of the Cascades is dominated by Mts. Baker and St. Helens. As Lewis and Clark passed down the river, Lewis wrote: "Three miles below the Image Canoe Island . . . we had a full view of the mountain. . . . (St. Helens) ; it rises in the form of a sugar loaf to a great height and is covered with snow." The rugged gorge where the Columbia cuts through the mighty mountains is the only natural break through a 2,000 mile stretch of the Cascades and Sierra Nevada.

At Vancouver, oldest settlement in the state, the Covington House is thought to be the oldest in Washington. Another place of interest is the former home of Ulysses S. Grant. At Vancouver is the monumental statue of the "Pioneer Mother," in memory of "all the brave mothers of the frontier." A restoration of Old Fort Vancouver is rich in memories of the grand old master of the region, Dr. John McLoughlin, and the stirring days of the Hudson's Bay Company dominion.

Longview was the first completely planned community of the entire Northwest. Although far from the ocean, it is a deepwater port on the Columbia. Another planned community is Ryderwood, a renowned retirement center.

The west coast of Washington is a fascinating, uncluttered, uncrowded stretch of scenic interest. The twenty-eight mile length of Long Beach is said to be the world's most extensive stretch of hard packed sand, where automobiles drive as though on the highway. Along the many sandy shores, shellers, clamers and simple hikers relish the joys of the seascape. Occasionally one may stop to pick up one of the Japanese glass fishing floats, large or small, that arrive on the shores after safe journeys, sometimes from Japan itself.

Mighty Monarch—Rainier

Towering Mount Rainier pushes a snowy head above the clouds and beckons more visitors than any other attraction in Washington. It is, in fact, one of the principal tourist attractions of the nation.

Soaring to the highest point in that state—14,410 feet—the mountain cradles the creeping, moaning, white bulk of twenty-six glaciers, holds sixty-two lakes in its hollows and provides streams and cliffs for the splash of thirty-four waterfalls.

Contrasting with the great bulk of the mountain, tiny mountain flowers nestle in the sunlight, often just under frowning lids of glacier ice. These delicate, enchanting blooms include the fragile avalanche lily, western anemone, mountain buttercup, mimulus, gentian and many more. Wapiti elk have moved into the region, and those dwellers of the crags, mountain goats, may often be seen. Fortunate observers may catch a fleeting glimpse of mountain lion, bobcat or even coyote.

Fishing, mountaineering, hiking, nature study, just plain looking, and skiing in season are all part of the tremendous attraction of the region. Paradise Inn is one of the nation's best-known centers of hospitality.

Paradise is a fitting place to leave this hasty excursion into the past and present of Washington State, for almost without exception the proud residents, no matter in what part of the state they live, contend that they have indeed found their paradise on earth.

PARADISE VALLEY
AND MT. RAINIER

Handy Reference Section

You Have A Date With History

1592—Apostolos Valerianos (Juan de Fuca) said to have found strait named in his honor

1774—Juan Perez coasts the shoreline, sights Olympics

1775—Heceta and Quadra, land on coast, take possession for Spain

1778—Captain James Cook names Cape Flattery, surveys coast

1787—Captain C. W. Barkley finds and names Strait of Juan de Fuca

1790—Manuel Quimper takes possession at Neah Bay

1791—Spain begins settlement at Neah Bay, soon abandoned

1792—Captain Robert Gray discovers Columbia River; Captain George Vancouver discovers Puget Sound

1805—Lewis and Clark party reaches coast

1810—Spokane House established by North West Fur Company

1811—Fort Okanogan established

1813—North West Company purchases Astor properties

1818—Fort Nez Perce (Walla Walla) built by North West Company; British and U. S. agree to joint occupancy of the region

1821—North West and Hudson's Bay Companies unite

1825—Dr. John McLoughlin begins "reign" at Fort Vancouver

1836—Marcus and Narcissa Whitman establish Waiilatpu

1843—First large settlers group crosses Oregon Trail

1846—Most of Oregon Territory becomes U. S.

1847—Massacre at Waiilatpu

1848—Oregon Territory created

1850—Olympia founded

1851—Seattle founded

1853—Washington Territory established

1855—Indian wars begin

1861—Territorial University opens

1864—First Mercer girls arrive at Seattle

1872—Spokane founded

1889—Statehood

1892—Washington State University founded

1909—Alaska-Yukon-Pacific Exposition, Seattle

1917—Lake Washington ship canal completed

1928—Capitol building completed, Olympia

1941—Grand Coulee completed

1944—Hanford develops atomic potential

1962—Century Twenty-One Exposition, Seattle

1965—Severe earthquake damages eastern Washington

State Flag

Marcus Whitman Pioneer missionary; built a mission with H. H. Spalding for the Indians at Waiilatpu, near Fort Walla Walla

THE SEAL OF THE STATE OF WASHINGTON ·1889·

State Seal

CANADA

John Jacob Astor His Pacific Fur Company built Fort Okanogan in 1811; the fur-trading post was one of the first settlements

Lummi Ind. Res.   Mt. Baker
Orcas I.   • Bellingham
San Juan I.   • Anacortes
Lopez I.
Cape Flattery
Skagit River
Strait of Juan de Fuca
Glacier Peak
Sawtooth Ridge
Okanogan River
Columbia River

Franklin D. Roosevelt Lake
Colville Ind. Res.
Grand Coulee Dam
Spokane Ind. Res.
Spokane •
• Opportunity

KETTLE RIVER RANGE

• Port Angeles
Olympic Nat'l. Park
• Everett

OLYMPIC MOUNTAINS
Rain Forest   • Seattle
Bremerton •
Quinault Ind. Res.   • Kent

Puget Sound

Chelan Range
Entiat Mountains

Moses Coulee

Wenatchee Mountains
• Wenatchee

• Moses Lake

IDAHO

Pacific Ocean

Hoquiam
Grays Harbor   • Aberdeen
Chehalis Ind. Res.
Centralia •
Willapa Bay
Willapa Hills

OLYMPIA ✪
Puyallup

CASCADE RANGE
Wenatchee River
Ginkgo Petrified For.

COLUMBIA BASIN
Columbia River

• Pullman
Snake River

• Tacoma

Mt. Ranier Nat'l. Park
U.S. Atomic Energy Commission Res.
Yakima •
• Hanford
Richland •

State Bird: Willow Goldfinch
• Longview
Mt. Adams
Yakima Valley
Yakima Ind. Res.
Yakima River
• Pasco
Kennewick •
Blue Mts.
• Walla Walla

Ft. Vancouver Nat'l. Mon.
Bonneville Dam
Horse Heaven Hills
McNary Dam
Whitman Nat'l. Mon.

State Flower: Coastal Rhododendron
Vancouver •
The Dalles Dam
Columbia River
OREGON

WASHINGTON

Instant Facts

Became 42nd state November 11, 1889
Capital—Olympia, founded 1850
State Bird—Willow goldfinch
State Flower—Rhododendron macrophyllium
State Tree—Western hemlock (Tsuga Heterophylla)
State Song—"Washington, My Home," by Helen Davis
Descriptive Name—The Evergreen State
Area—68,192 square miles
Greatest Length (north to south)—230 miles
Greatest Width (east to west)—340 miles
Highest Point—14,410 feet, Mount Rainier
Lowest Point—Sea level
Highest Recorded Temperature—118° (Ice Harbor Dam)
Lowest Recorded Temperature—minus 42° (near Deer Park)
Population—3,175,000 (1965 estimate)
Population Density—40.8 persons per square mile (1960)
Principal Cities—Seattle   557,087 (1960 census)
                 Spokane   181,608
                 Tacoma   147,979
                 Yakima   43,284
                 Everett   40,304
                 Bellingham   34,688
                 Vancouver   32,464

Thinkers, Doers, Fighters

People of renown who have been associated with Washington

Bennett, John
Boeing, William
Clark, William
Crosby, Harry Lillis (Bing)
Dubilier, William
Garry (Chief)
Grant, Ulysses Simpson
Hallshallakeen (Chief Joseph, the Younger)
Lewis, Meriweather
Livingston, Mary
MacDonald, Betty
McLoughlin, John

Munsel, Patrice
Parrington, Vernon Louis
Pickett, George
Roethke, Theodore
Seattle (Chief)
Sohon, Gustave
Taylor, Moulton B.
Tobey, Mark
Whitman, Marcus
Whitman, Narcissa
Wurdemann, Audrey

Annual Events

March-April—Daffodil Festival, Tacoma
May—Northwest Blossomtime Festival
May—Lilac Week, Spokane
May—Armed Forces Day Celebration, Oak Harbor
May—Washington State Apple Blossom Festival, Wenatchee
May—Rhododendron Festival, Port Townsend
June—Lummi-Stomish Indian Water Carnival, Bellingham
June—Sun Festival, Ephrata
June—Kon Tiki Raft Race and Water Carnival, Kelso
July—Salt Water Fishing Derby, Westport
July—Pow-Wow Parade and Rodeo, Toppenish
July—Olympia Games, Olympia
July—Loggerodeo Fourth of July Celebration, Sedro Woolley
July—Tri-City Water Follies, Richland, Pasco, Kennewick
July—Pacific Northwest Arts and Crafts Fair, Seattle
July—Old Fashioned Celebration, Prosser
July—Capital Lake Fair, Olympia
July—Heather Cup Races, Bellingham
July-August—Seafair, Seattle
August—Salmon Fishing Derbies, Port Townsend
August—Amputee Golf Tournament, Spokane
August—Town Barbecue, Packwood
September—State Day Celebration, Prosser
September—Ellensburg Rodeo, Ellensburg
September—Frontier-Days and Southeastern Washington Fair, Walla Walla
December—Christmas Isle, Olympia

Governors

Elisha P. Ferry, 1889–1893
John H. McGraw, 1893–1901
Henry McBride, 1901–1905
Albert E. Mead, 1905–1909
Samuel G. Cosgrove, 1909–
Marion E. Hay, 1909–1913
Ernest Lister, 1913–1919
Louis F. Hart, 1919–1925

Roland H. Hartley, 1925–1933
Clarence D. Martin, 1933–1941
Arthur B. Langlie, 1941–1945
Mon C. Walgren, 1945–1949
Arthur B. Langlie, 1949–1957
Albert D. Rosellini, 1957–1965
Daniel J. Evans, 1965–

INDEX